Tales of
Norfolk Folk

The Author   (Photo: *Terry Burchell*)

Tales of Norfolk Folk

Including the Royal Cooper Story

Robert Bagshaw

To Nicholas, my son

Cover Illustration: Hunsett Mill, River Ant.
Photo: The Author.

By the Same Author:
Poppies To Paston.
Toothy Goes To War.
Norfolk Remembered.
More Memories of Norfolk.
Echoes of Old Norfolk.
A Norfolk Chronicle.

ISBN   Hardback: 0 900616 63 6
        Softback: 0 900616 64 4

Printed and published by
Geo. R. Reeve Ltd., 9-11 Town Green, Wymondham, Norfolk.

CONTENTS

ILLUSTRATIONS

ILLUSTRATIONS (continued)

PROLOGUE

All Because of Jenny

It was quite a decent day for March – not exactly sunny, but dry and with just a hint of warmth in the air. Just the sort of day, I thought, to go and see Jenny.

Jenny and I share an association going back something like half a century. Being without transport apart from her elderly bicycle, she only visits me when somebody brings her, but I make the trip in her direction from time to time. She still lives in the cottage in which she was born, in a village which surely must have changed as little in her lifetime as any other in Norfolk. Being well away from any suggestion of a dual carriageway and, at the same time, sufficiently remote from the more northerly hotspots to offer little attraction to second-home buyers, it has remained almost free of both commuters and computers. Indeed, if the place could speak, one gets the feeling that it would express its wish to have no truck with either.

Edith at the Post Office feels the same way about modern information technology, having sold stamps and paid out pensions without it for as long as anybody can remember, but this could well bring about her downfall if her masters have their way. Even then, I fancy she might carry on selling Oxo cubes and boiled sweets from her little front room.

There is no real centre of population in the village. In various places there are terraces of four or five houses, but most folk live in odd ones or twos, mostly with a parcel of land, sprinkled around the parish. Jenny is one of those, and at one time she kept a cow – her butter was something out of this world – but now she settles for a yard full of very free-range hens.

Jenny is one of the few people who have never felt the inclination to buy a television set. She listens to the news on an extremely ancient wireless set on the table by her armchair and, when she wants to listen to special music, she plays very old-fashioned records on an equally old-fashioned wind-up gramophone.

Even more surprising, perhaps, is the fact that she has always resisted attempts from many quarters to have a telephone. She had several confrontations on the matter with what she calls 'them Social people,' who then switched their attack to her need to wear round her neck one of those emergency buttons which would summon help when needed. Eventually she acquiesced – but only to please them. She never wears it.

"I've got it in a safe place," she said. "It's in my dressing table drawer upstairs."

Because of her lack of a telephone, I would always arrive unheralded, but the welcome was always warm and immediate. On this occasion, however, it was as I arrived outside her cottage that I realised that something was amiss. The place just didn't look right. It was the windows that did it. Gone were the white net curtains, so handy to peep through from inside the house. Gone were the geraniums which seemed to flower unceasingly on the windowsills. And gone was the aspidistra which stood on a table inside her large downstairs window. Some of the windows looked out in their nakedness, whilst others were covered with sheets of newspaper pinned to the inside of the frames.

Then, as I walked by the side of the cottage to the backyard, I realised that the hens were silent, their cackling replaced by the sound of a rhythmic beat. As I reached the yard my heart fell, for there was Jenny, beating a carpet. She was Spring Cleaning!

She turned at the sound of my approach, and there it was – the biggest, most welcoming of smiles beaming at me from under her mob-cap. I tried to apologise for interrupting her, but she would have none of it.

"Dew yew come indoors," she said. "It'll dew me no harm to take a break. I've been at it since nigh on six this morning and I reckon it'll be nice to have someone to share a cup o' tea with. Dew yew come in."

And, as she spoke, she did what every countrywoman does when somebody calls unexpectedly – she began to untie her apron strings. No matter whether you catch them baking or at the wash-tub, the first thing they do is slide their fingers to the knots, undo them and cast the garment aside. No matter that the apron is far cleaner than what it hides. It just isn't right to receive company in your apron.

"So you're Spring Cleaning?" I said, stating the obvious.

"Thass right," said Jenny. "We're all at it. We're all a-cleanin' down for Easter."

10

I couldn't help wondering why the phrase 'cleaning up' refers to routine housework, whilst 'cleaning down' is always reserved for the Spring onslaught.

But Jenny was a woman with a mission. One of her neighbours, she said, claimed to have already finished 'cleaning down.'

"Well," said Jenny, "she only had her curtains down a week, so she must have cut a few corners."

She had no time for the modern 'spray and wipe' type of cleaning, and as for the Vicar's wife, who preferred to send her carpets to the laundry: "I don't hold with them methods – 'dew 'em yerself,' I say, 'and then yew know they're done'."

Eventually, I took my leave of Jenny and left her to continue her crusade of cleanliness and, on the way home, I ruminated on the past. Did they not teach us, all those years ago, that cleanliness is next to godliness? Is it not natural that all those countrywomen like Jenny should cherish a reputation for cleanliness? Some people are proud of their wealth, others of their double glazing or their flower beds packed tight with the latest F1 hybrids. Why, then, shouldn't the Jennys of this world be proud of their cleanliness?

Yet, the thought of Jenny refused to go away, and I recalled, as I have done on many occasions over the years, one room which could do with a little 'cleaning down.' It is the room we have always, rather laughingly, called my study. It is, in truth, rather more the receptacle for all sorts of books and papers that I have accumulated over the years – rubbish of no interest to anybody else, but a veritable treasure trove to me. There are letters – not the kind that a computer churns out in unseemly numbers, but real letters from real people who have taken the trouble to write to me. There are files packed with pieces of paper bearing notes on topics which might be useful if ever I felt like working on another book.

At this point I feel that you, dear reader, may already be ahead of me. If you are reading this in print you will know that Yes, I made the mistake of starting to read those papers, and No, I did not 'clean down' my study.

If you enjoy what lies ahead in this book, I shall be pleased – and forever grateful to dear, houseproud Jenny.

1

The Way We Were

CHAPTER 1

Twentieth Century Feudalism

For many years until recently I have enjoyed a fine friendship with a dear man not only twenty years my senior but coming from a somewhat dissimilar background. Ben Burgess lived in a world of agriculture spreading far beyond the family estate at Howe and Brooke. I had little direct knowledge of farming, limited to what was normal for a youngster to acquire while growing up in the Norfolk countryside. But, of course, it was the Old School that had something to do with it, for, like Horatio Nelson before us, we were both Old Pastonians. I cannot recall where and when we first met, but somehow we 'took a shine to each other' and realised that it was fun being together and recalling memories of our respective pasts.

He invited me to have lunch with him, firstly at the Norfolk Club but, ever afterwards, in the considerably less formal atmosphere of his office. It was a very large room, which was just as well, for it was tightly packed from floor to ceiling with the vast collection of Nelson memorabilia which he had spent a lifetime acquiring and which, happily, is now assembled in its own museum at Yarmouth. I chuckled inwardly as I noticed two correspondence trays side by side on a table, one marked 'BUSINESS' containing just three single sheets of paper and the other inscribed 'MINE' piled two feet high with an assortment of literature. Then, in the corner, there was a fridge which, at the appropriate time, was opened to reveal a cheese board, with a tempting array of cheeses, and one of the most succulent game pies I have ever seen.

That was the setting where, over the years, we took lunch together, with the warmth of the inevitable glass of claret adding to the glowing feeling of mutual inner contentment. And, all the while, we talked - though I have to say that it was Ben who did most of the talking. Unlike the Queen Mother, he just missed out on his century, but he had such a fertile memory and could recount to me tales of things which I had merely read about but which he himself had actually experienced. What a wonderful book he could have produced if only he had been able to gather all his memories together!

Here, in fact, was a man who had witnessed at first hand, and could actively recall, many of the demands and responsibilties imposed upon countryfolk by the near-defunct age of feudalism. I had read about it, but Ben had seen it!

There was, for instance, the time when Ben and his brother Edward, both boarders at Sir William Paston's School in North Walsham, were two of a number of boys struck down with chicken pox. The year was 1914, and the boys had spent the last part of the summer term in the sanatorium, probably sufficiently isolated to be unaware of all the talk of impending war. When the term ended the other boys all went home, but it was decided that Edward and Ben needed a few more days before they could be considered completely free from infection. It is thought that Mother was not in favour of the idea of bringing them home to infect everybody in the household, so the sanatorium was closed and the boys were moved down into the long dormitory of the School House.

On either the last day of July or the first of August, they went to bed in the normal way at about 9 o'clock and proceeded to sleep the sleep of the just, not expecting to wake until Matron's voice would disturb their slumbers at 7 o'clock the next morning. But it was not Matron's voice that Ben first heard. He remembers being in that halfway stage between dream and consciousness when he became aware of a strange metallic tinkling sound - not the sort of sound usually heard in the 'long dorm'. He opened his eyes to investigate its source and found himself looking face-to-face at a strange man sitting in the next bed and not more than three or four feet away from him. It took only seconds to realise that the man was a soldier and, what is more, a Norfolk Yeomanryman at that. The tinkling was caused by his efforts at cleaning the strip of chain mail on the shoulder of his tunic with his button stick and an old toothbrush.

The soldier signalled to Ben to be quiet, and a cautious look round the dormitory revealed no less than nine more of his like, mostly asleep. And this is where the feudal system comes in, for the soldier was a second lieutenant who, on taking his commission, had contracted to find his own servant and a couple of horses. That was what the County Sheriffs had demanded of the soldiers whom they had been obliged to recruit since Plantagenet times in

16

Ben Burgess

a call to arms which had been going on for 500 years, when the King decided to go to war.

The second lieutenant was, in fact, young Cyril Case of Binham (and later of Harpley). He had received his telegram earlier that day and had collected his father's stockman/groom and a couple of father's riding horses. Then he and his 'servant' proudly donned their distinctive blue and silver uniforms and set out for their assembly point at North Walsham.

It might seem a long way from Binham to North Walsham, but Cyril Case and his groom were used to long days in the saddle together. Every young farmer in West Norfolk hunted with the West Norfolk Foxhounds and, if the meet was a long way from home, they had to take three horses with them. No mount would do his rider justice if he had ridden ten miles before the Hunt moved off. Cyril Case and his groom were amongst the last to answer the feudal system's call to arms, and he later expressed his delight at being offered a grammar school boy's bed after the ride from Binham. He had expected to spend the rest of the night on the floor of the stable.

Incidentally, by the time the boys returned to school in September 1914, the Norfolk Regiment were in the town - the Cyclist Battalion. It was a stirring sight to see 500 soldiers in khaki and puttees cycle up the Norwich Road. They had to be four abreast, of course, just as if they were marching on their feet. There was very little room for the other traffic. Horses and carts had to take refuge in gateways when they met the Norfolk Cyclist Battalion!

The second surviving piece of feudalism which Ben recalled to me was far removed from the glamour of donning fancy uniforms and parading through the streets. It was an arduous, filthy duty, based upon the Manorial system's stipulation that every man, be he freeman or villein, must willingly give free service and days of work to his lord. It was, in fact, the annual coaling-up of the landlord's house - in this case Brooke Hall, that expensive pile which the Holmes family had built to keep up with the Joneses when they could no longer afford it.

"It took a trainload of coals to keep it warm through the winter and to feed the kitchen ranges, too, throughout the year." At least that was the opinion expressed in the village. Certainly, even if it was not exactly a train load of 'Newstead Brights' which came into Trowse station towards the end of July, it was at least several

In 1901, Major H. A. Barclay of Hanworth Hall was designated to raise the King's Own Regiment of Norfolk Imperial Yeomanry. North Walsham was the base for Squadron B of the Regiment, seen here parading in the Market Place

truckloads. All the tenants supplied transport, and the Burgesses accepted it as a traditional obligation to their landlord and Lord of the Manor. The brothers always went out of their way to help the Estate, for they had a benevolent attitude towards their ageing landlord and appreciated his financial difficulties.

Young Ben found it difficult to understand at the time. He just accepted it as one of those events in the farming year like harvest suppers, Christmas, Easter and Bungay May Fair.

All the coal arrived at Trowse in truckloads of 6 and 8 tons, and each truck was usually cleared by three wagons, one from each of the major farms, and off-loaded to maintain stocks at bunker points. Loose coal, to be shovelled from rail trucks onto wagons and unloaded again at the farms, was at best a dirty job which could not have been eagerly anticipated by the team-men involved. Yet it was all carried out with pride. Normally, there were very few four-horse teams to be seen on the road to Norwich, but on this day it was different. A four-horse team added prestige to both team-men and employer, so the men got busy fixing brasses on the bridles, braiding the horses' tails, forelocks and manes and adding the final touch with coloured ribbons.

No, indeed. The annual coaling-up of the big house of the Lord of the Manor was not just another chore. The team-men from the whole estate turned it into a social occasion, working together with a will and, when the job was done, gathering at the *Pineapple* for merriment and as much beer as any man could drink. Then, at the end of the day, they would struggle on board their wagons - and leave it to the horses to find the way home.

From those stories of the final days of feudalism in his early boyhood, I suppose it was only natural that Ben's memory should take the short step to a man around whom the entire feudal system revolved - The Old Squire. The man in question in Ben's life was Charles Fellowes of Shotesham Park.

Born in the year of Waterloo, after the battle, he lived until 1914, dying just before the outbreak of the First World War, and he was, in Ben's words, "probably the last of the great intolerant squires of Norfolk."

The world of 'The Old Squire' was an uncomplicated place, for every man knew - and accepted - his position in the scheme of things. No doubt the King was at the head of it, closely followed by the nobility and then the Squirearchy and a few - a very few - landless gentlemen. There was then a very large gap between

Coal wagons being shunted into sidings ready for their contents to be collected by the Lord of the Manor's tenant farmers

these and the local farmers, mostly his own tenants. Perhaps he would have liked to forget that this group existed, but there were times when, in the dim fastnesses of his mind, he realised that his very existence depended upon their rents. Hence he had a habit of acknowledging his own tenants, and he condescended to give Ben's father 'the seal of the day' when they met in the village.

"My father knew," said Ben, "what a terrible old tyrant he was, but he respected the Old Squire for what he was, the last living reminder of the feudal system. So he pitied him, rather than blaming him, for his tyrannical actions."

The children were adjured to greet him with a clearly enunciated "Good morning, Squire" whenever they met him on the road, which was very frequently, for he rode out most mornings and, once a week, could be seen coming through Howe after taking a detour through what was, to him, the "strange territory" of the Holmes Estate.

The Old Squire was never alone. He was always on a well-groomed cob and followed at a respectful horse's length by a groom on another, but smaller, cob. It was unthinkable, of course, that master and groom should ever have anything to say to one another, short of a dire emergency, or that they should ride side-by-side. It was unthinkable, too, that small children by the

21

roadside in their governess cart should be acknowledged by the spoken word. The most the Burgess children ever got was a slight inclination of the head or a two-inch lift of the hunting crop. "But that," said Ben, "did not deter us from our duty."

The last time they saw The Old Squire was in 1913 at the traditional Boxing Day meet of the Norwich Staghounds on Howe Common. He was 99 years old and the centre of attention.

"I can see his low distinctive top hat even now," said Ben, "among the other hunting headgear, and I suppose it was the only time the groom caught up with him, for there he was, dismounted and holding his master's cob by the bridle. We were in our governess cart on the perimeter of a melée of horses, hounds and humans. After the war, the Norwich Staghounds again held their Boxing Day meet on Howe Common for a year or two, but it was never the same again without The Old Squire."

CHAPTER 2

Kill or Cure at Kelling

It was on a bitterly cold January day in 1913 that Jack Barrett went on a very strange journey to an even stranger place, and it was a journey that was to stay in his memory for the rest of his life.

Jack was a real Fen Tiger, living much of his early life in the Feltwell Fens and relishing the freedom and liberty of his surroundings, as did all the old fenmen. He was a man of the great outdoors, strong and hardy, fit as a fiddle. At least, that was what he thought, until he was suddenly stricken down by a disease which was rife throughout the country in the early 1900s. It was 'consumption,' correctly knows as pulmonary tuberculosis or, in the more recent days of initialisation, simply as T.B.

The death rate from the disease was such that many considered it to be incurable, but there were others who believed that much could be done, particularly for the many victims living in poverty-stricken city areas, by means of a regular diet and pure fresh air. Hence it came about that Kelling Sanatorium was built and opened to its first fifty or so patients in 1903.

They had picked the 32-acre site, about a mile from Holt on the road to Cromer, with great care, for it was sheltered on three sides by pinewoods and near enough to the sea to benefit from the winds that came in from that quarter. It was dry and bracing, and eminently suitable for a system of open-air treatment. For that was what they provided – a degree of open-airness which came as a shock for most patients encountering it for the first time. The administrative block was conventional enough, but the patients' sleeping quarters comprised a collection of wooden cubicles, filled in on only three sides and with merely a pair of curtains that could be pulled across the open side at night. Many were the tales of having to get out of bed to shake the snow from the bedclothes! But there was recompense in that each cubicle stood on a turntable, which made it possible for the structure to be moved round to face the best of weather conditions.

This, then, was Jack Barrett's destination when he set out on that icy-cold journey in January 1913. Just twenty-one years old, he had been passed from one doctor to another under the auspices of the recently-established Norfolk Insurance Committee, and then came the news that a bed awaited him at Kelling. He was told

The main concourse of Kelling Sanatorium in its pinewood setting, 1910.

The chalets in which patients slept, irrespective of the weather. No doors –
simply curtains which could be drawn at night.

which train to catch to Holt, where transport would be waiting to take him on the last mile or so of his journey.

"I shall never forget that journey from Holt station," he said. "The cab, provided by the local jobmaster, was an ancient contraption used for only one purpose – to carry patients to and from the sanatorium."

And disaster was soon to strike. Having endured a long rail journey in an unheated compartment, it is not surprising that his feet were extremely cold, and, in order to stimulate the circulation, he began to stamp them on the floor of the cab. It was a near-fatal mistake. There was a crash, the bottom of the cab fell out onto the road and, unable to attract the attention of the driver outside on his box, he found himself having to run inside the cab until the approach to the railway bridge compelled the cab-horse to slacken its speed.

The rest of the journey was completed up on the box beside the cab driver. "And," said Jack, "he refused to give me any rebate on the fare!"

Kelling, at that time, boasted of seventy beds although, by 1937, there were 170 within the complex. The new arrival was conducted to the appropriate area, where patients who had been there for some time were quick to inform him that the cubicles were bitterly cold and the treatment was 'kill or cure.' He was soon to experience those facts for himself.

He was also not long in learning that every single facet of life at Kelling was conducted with a never-wavering consistency. The night nurse popped in and took his temperature at half past six in the morning, after which he went to wash and shave in an open shed in the north wing. Then it was back to his cubicle to make his bed – four to six blankets according to season, with a large stone hot water bottle for the really severe weather. When it came to consistency, however, catering excelled all else, for it was organised so that whatever the patients had on the first Monday of the year they would get for the next 51 Mondays, and so on right through the week.

Patients were expected to do a certain amount of work, according to their physical condition. Instructors were employed to teach patients certain skills and the whole thing was co-ordinated under the mantle of the grandly-named Kelling Sanatorium Industries.

Those not working were required to take an hour's exercise

along the Cromer Road – the women in the morning and the men in the afternoon. The remainder of the time they had to sit in the chalets, resting. Rest was the main watchword. Every patient had to rest for an hour both before and after meals, "just resting". There was no reading or knitting or anything like that – "just resting." There was no way a patient could miss those rest periods, for each was ushered in by a nurse running round the compound, ringing a bell and shouting, "Legs up."

Even those who worked on a daily basis had time off on Saturday afternoons, ostensibly for exercise. For most of them it was a hike to Bodham *White Hart,* the only pub within walking distance that would serve them. People were scared of consumption, and in those days the townsfolk of Holt were not keen on the sanatorium.

Sunday was visiting day and, as such, the quietest day of the week, for everybody was so far away from home, especially the patients from Leicester, for whom their city had made arrangements to share the Kelling facilities. The Midland & Great Northern Railway never indulged in running trains on Sundays, and there was no other form of transport, for buses were still just a dream of the future.

"At that time," said Jack, "the Sabbath at Kelling was dismal. One looked forward to bedtime on a Sunday; with hot bottle filled and snug beneath the blankets, you dreamed of the cosy home to which you were hoping to go back."

Thursday night was weigh night for all the patients who were up and about. Matron was clerk of the scales and pronounced her judgement after each weigh-in, with an admonishment where she thought it was necessary. If a patient had gained weight, he was given more work to do. If he had lost a little, he was given an extra spoonful of porridge, together with a wigging from Matron. It was this last ordeal that the men feared most, but they soon found a way to thwart her. If one of them had the idea that he had lost half a pound, into his pocket would go a pound or so of lead, handed from patient to patient.

As one would expect, the patients at Kelling were a mixed bunch, for consumption was no respecter of persons. Some would get better and go home – back to the same conditions they had left; they would carry on for a time and then break down again. Others – and there were many of them – never went home. Those who came out on top were the ones who made the best of a bad job, stuck to the treatment and, when it was all over, walked back to Holt station and pocketed the one-and-sixpence they were given for the cab fare.

Jack Barrett was one such man, and he never allowed himself to forget the debt he owed to the people who had brought him back to health.

"The medical and nursing staff," he said, "were of the stuff that heroes are made. They might be blue with cold, chilled to the bone, yet were always smiling and cheerful. The pay might be poor, but they put everything into the job in hand. As the years pass, my admiration grows greater, for with all the discomfort and grouses involved, by their skill and care they put me on my feet again to take my place in the outside world."

Jack went back to being a Fen Tiger, back to places like Brandon Creek and Hockwold cum Wilton, with the freedom and liberty he cherished. Later he moved over to the south of the county, which is where our paths crossed. He was a wondrous story-teller, and there were many of us who urged him to put his memories down on paper. The years went by, and then, just as we were giving up hope – for he had passed his seventy-second birthday – *Tales from the Fens* appeared in the bookshops, closely followed by *More Tales from the Fens* and *A Fenman's Story.* He had made up for lost time, and, at the time of his death in 1974 at the age of 83, there was already another manuscript ready for the printers. With the help of his friend, Percy Garrod, *East Anglian Folklore* appeared in 1976 to complete a splendid quartet of local volumes.

One is left wondering whether any of that would have been possible had it not been for the dedication of the good folk of Kelling.

Way Back When

Life today's so different from the way it used to be,
When Grace was said at table, with dripping toast for tea.
Gym slips were the fashion, girdles of different hues,
Itchy woollen stockings and baby Peggy shoes.

Homes were lit by gaslight and so was every street,
The respected local Bobby plodded on his beat.
Washing Day with Hudson's soap, a chore for every Monday,
Children went to school in church each and every Sunday.

Merry's bread or Ashworth's, spread with raspberry jam,
Chimney sweeps, lantern slides, and the cat's meat man.
Amami night on Friday, tin bath and lifebuoy soap,
Rousing Temperance Meetings at the Band of Hope.

Charabancs with canvas tops, trains that ran on steam;
To be wooed by Valentino was every female's dream.
It wasn't all that rosy for life was harder then,
But it's fun to reminisce at times the days of way back when.

Lines writen by an unknown Norwich Woman.

'... and the cat's meat man,' otherwise known as 'Pussy's Butcher.'

'Charabancs with canvas tops.' Norwich Deaf Outing to Clacton,
July 21st 1928

CHAPTER 4

Taking A Bath -
And Other Matters

I doubt whether there are many people who, in this present age of luxury and convenience, would consider the act of taking a bath worthy of a mention in their diary of significant happenings. It is, after all, an integral part of one's daily life, carried out with a minimum of preparation and with no great disruption of one's other activities.

To begin with, there stands the plumbed-in bath, permanently ensconced in its own special room. There is the water, in unlimited quantity and at whatever temperature one desires, readily available at the turn of a tap. And there, on a shelf, are all the delicately scented concoctions to add to the water to enable one to "relax in a hot herbal bath with its secret blend of herbs and minerals and let it melt away the aches and pains of everyday living." Finally, of course, there is the central heating, silently chuntering away to ensure that one's unclothed form is not subjected to any drop of temperature in the surrounding air.

But it was not always like that - far from it! Many of the more mature members of present-day society still readily recall - indeed, how could they ever forget? - the rigours and tortures of Bath Night (usually a Friday). In would come the tin bath from its hook in the outhouse where it had hung for the rest of the week, to take its place on the floor in front of the kitchen fire. Then, in came the hot water from the steaming copper in the scullery, brought in to fill the bath by a human chain of buckets and jugs. Bath Night was not only a trial of human stamina but, at the same time, a marvel of logistical organisation. And, all the while, the only fragrances which wafted around us as we strove to scrub our bodies clean came from the block of rock-hard Lifebuoy Soap and the even stronger Carbolic. One other product also lives in blessed memory - a substance known simply as Monkey Brand. Strictly speaking, it was not soap, but rather a solid block of abrasive material intended for use in cleaning such things as paintwork, marble slabs and bicycles. Many of us, however, can vouch for

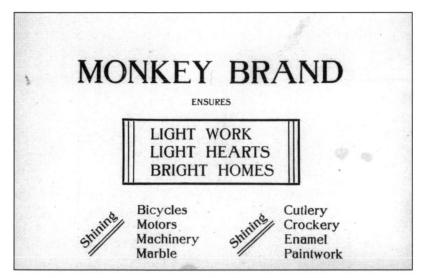

MONKEY BRAND

ENSURES

LIGHT WORK
LIGHT HEARTS
BRIGHT HOMES

Shining Bicycles
Motors
Machinery
Marble

Shining Cutlery
Crockery
Enamel
Paintwork

The everyday cleaner for most things, including small boys' knees!

its efficacy in removing from small boys' knees the ingrained dirt which tended to accumulate during the course of a day spent climbing trees and kneeling in hedgerows and on grassy banks to observe the activity in Nature's underworld.

Lilias Rider Haggard, that much-revered Norfolk writer, committed her impressions of Bath Night, country style, to the pages of her diary. It was in 1936, when she and her companion, Ethel, had taken over a cottage and were busy bringing it into a condition befitting the occupancy of two maiden ladies.

"Last night," she wrote, "I had a bath, a thing not to be undertaken lightly or inadvisably. It takes place in the kitchen and entails great preparation. First, Ethel modestly drapes all apertures with teacloths, as we have not yet achieved curtains. I enter an abode that looks as if I am preparing to gas myself, and ladle boiling water from the copper into a tin saucer. Its surface looks doubtful, and I get in and try not to remember all the times I have used it as a pond for young ducks. A slight miscalculation as to how much displacement room my form requires results in a flood which, owing to the slope of the floor, fortunately mostly flows out under the back door. Finally I conclude and leave the kitchen swimming in water and fog-like with steam - but I have HAD a bath!"

Poor Lilias! What a shock it must have been to her maidenly susceptibilities! Yet she was vastly more fortunate than the great mass of countryfolk who, all over the county, engaged in the Friday ritual of 'taking the waters.'

Three ladies of my acquaintance, all of them - if I dare bring myself to say so - having now achieved a certain degree of maturity, have cast their minds back to the past and collectively provided an authentic picture of family life in the spartan days of their respective childhoods.

Spare a thought, for instance, for Ann Thrower. Ann is a farmer's daughter, the youngest of fourteen children born to Royal and Olive Cooper of Swannington, and the memories of Bath Night have stayed with her throughout her life. Not for Ann and her siblings was there the warmth of the kitchen fire to combat the cold, for their Friday night routine took place in one of the smaller sheds out in the yard. The shed had a very ill-fitting door and many other points of entry for the winter winds, but the reason for its choice as a bathroom was the fact that it contained a boiler in which the water could be heated. Each Friday night the copper would be lit - "old rubber boots made the best fuel," says Ann - and wooden clothes-horses with blankets and old coats draped over them would be stood in strategic positions to give protection from the draughts which whistled through the door. Then the old tin bath would be brought in, placed in front of the copper and filled with hot water. It was not a question of clean water for each child - merely another pail of hot water from the boiler to re-heat what was already in there, with an occasional bucketful taken out to prevent an overflow.

It is true that, with such a large family, there was a great age difference between oldest and youngest, and some had already moved to other places, but there were still plenty in the queue battling for pride of place while the water still retained some of its initial freshness.

"It wasn't too bad in the summer," says Ann, "but in winter we had to wrap up in our coats and scarves when going for a bath as the shed was quite a way from the house. Then it would be a quick dash back to the house before you caught your death of cold."

It was at this point that Irene, Ann's oldest sister and 22 years her senior, took over the narrative, with a memory as clear as though the Bath Nights had taken place just the previous week.

"After our bath," she said, "we all had clean vests - mostly

The Cooper sisters, Irene (left) and Ann

hand-knitted woollen ones for winter, cotton interlock for summer - and clean flannelette nightdresses or shirts. We used to wear a lot more clothes than children do nowadays as most of the time we only had a fire in one room - unless it was a wet week and we had to have lines across another room to dry the washing. As well as a vest we had a chemise, then a liberty bodice and knickers with elastic at the knee - just right for tucking one's hankie in. Then in winter a flannelette petticoat, in summer a cotton one, and after this came last year's Sunday dress and a pinafore to keep it clean for school. We only changed our underwear once a week ('Disgusting,' my granddaughter would say) but even so, with sheets and towels, there was always a big pile for Washday."

In country households in those days each day of the week was set aside for a specific purpose and, just as Friday was Bath Night, so Monday, for as long as anybody could remember, had been Washday - the routine never varied. Shirts and similar garments had to be soaked and scrubbed with the housewife's favourite, Sunlight soap, before being put into the big copper and boiled

EQUATION:—
LABOUR LIGHT, CLOTHES WHITE = SUNLIGHT.

Sunlight Soap, the housewives' favourite for the Monday Wash.

34

with soda. Hence, as they had no village shop, they welcomed the visit, every few weeks, of a little old man with his pony and cart laden with a variety of household requisites. There were pots and pans, black-lead for the fire grates, white chalk stone for the hearth, Brasso for the door knobs, blue-bags for whitening and Robin starch for stiffening - and ample stocks of Sunlight soap and soda.

Whenever possible, they made use of the rainwater collected in the big butt by the door, and then the garments had to be rinsed twice in water from the same source - an unpleasant task in winter. The first rinse was not too bad, for they were still hot from the copper, but the second rinse, with ice frequently floating on the water, was distinctly uncomfortable.

"After this," says Irene, "they had to be carried through the garden to the orchard, where we had wire clothes lines from tree to tree. In frosty weather they used to be frozen stiff as soon as we got them on the line."

Nothing was wasted in those days if a second use could be found for it, and this applied every week to the water in the copper after the last of the sheets had been hung on the line. Ann's words will explain:

"We didn't have a lavatory in the house and, as it would have been a long, cold journey to the one outside, we had chamber pots under our beds. The girls had flowered ones and the boys had plain white. I well remember all the chamber pots being brought to the top of the stairs on the landing on Washday and being filled with boiling water left over after washing the sheets, to scald them out. Then my job would be to put them all back under the beds."

At this point it seems appropriate to introduce Jessie Webster, the last of my trio of nostalgia dispensers. Jess, like Irene, was a Great War baby, being born in Hethersett while her father was at the front, 'following the horses,' as a farrier in the Veterinary Corps. At the end of the War, he found employment as a blacksmith at Little Witchingham and Jess went to school at Swannington - the very same village where the Cooper family were living, though it seems they never met.

Jess, of course, remembers the horrors of Bath Night and Washday, and also her weekly task of scraping the tallow from their enamel candle holders which, with oil lamps the only other source of lighting, were in daily use.

"Another job," she told me, "was washing the chamber pots out in the hot soda water from the copper on Mondays and putting them outside to dry and air. Mum said hers were the prettiest in our row of houses - she said George's Mum across the way never washed hers!"

So it seems that the lowly chamber pot had become something of a status symbol! It is also readily apparent that George and his family were not held in very high regard when it came to matters of hygiene and personal cleanliness.

"When you opened the door," says Jess, "the fug came out and nearly laid you flat on your back."

In spite of this, however, they were "very nice people and well liked." Young George, in particular, enjoyed great popularity amongst his peers, largely because he was the proud owner of a phonograph, very much in the mould of the one portrayed in the old "His Master's Voice" picture. It played tubular records, each being issued in its own round cardboard box, and some of them would start with a voice saying, "This is an Edison Bell record." Jessie's favourite was a recording of a popular song of those times, "I Wouldn't Leave My Little Wooden Hut For You." George would sit in his front porch playing the phonograph, and Jessie and the other local youngsters would gather round to listen.

"We would put up with George's pong," says Jess, "as long as we could listen to those old songs."

Youngsters of today must find it difficult to understand how countryfolk of yesteryear managed to exist without so many of the conveniences that we now take for granted - such things as hot and cold running water, gas and electricity. Heating came from the kitchen range, with the luxury of an open fire in the sitting room on Sundays. The main lighting source was the paraffin lamp, which had to be cleaned on a daily basis. The wick had to be trimmed, the glass chimney polished and the globe dusted - all done first thing in the morning while there was good natural light. "The cleaner the lamp, the brighter the light," said Jessie's mother.

For moving about after dark, a lighted candle provided a flickering light, with one's hand crooked around its flame as one climbed the stairs to prevent it from being blown out. Then it would stand on the bedpost while one got undressed and ready for bed.

In the morning, even in the heavily-populated Cooper household, there would be no rush for the bathroom, for they had no such place. Their wash and brush up routine was carried out in the bedroom by bringing up hot water in a big china jug and pouring it into the handbasin which stood on the marble-topped washstand.

"Usually the jug and basin were quite pretty with flowers on the side," says Ann, "and if you were REALLY posh you could have your chamber pots to match. I don't remember ours matching," she says, "and we obviously weren't very posh because, instead of having a proper soap dish to put our soap in, we would use an old saucer."

It was, of course, the lack of a supply of running water that gave rise to the proliferation of outside lavatories standing in virtually every garden throughout the countryside, about which so much has already been written that further comment here is unnecessary. Suffice to say that, though they may have varied in form in accordance with their creator's imagination and the materials he had available, they all shared certain characteristics. They offered convenience without comfort and basic relief without beauty, though many owners sought to overcome that latter deficiency by means of a screen of hollyhocks in an effort to pretend it wasn't really there.

Within those walls there was, of course, no hint of anything resembling the soft-tissued, pastel-coloured toilet rolls of the present day - merely pages of a newspaper torn to a convenient size. In the Webster household, the task of preparing these fell to young Jess, who patiently made a hole in the corner of each sheet and threaded them on to a piece of string to be hung on a nail ready for use.

"The weekly magazine, *John Bull*, was just right," she says - "two pieces per page."

Pre-prepared paper, however, was not a luxury enjoyed by the Cooper family.

"I remember feeling quite 'lower class'," says Ann, "when I found out that my friend's family had their lavatory paper cut into squares and hung on a nail. Ours used to lie on the seat bench and we had to tear our own! But," she added, "we did have one up on them as we had a two-seated lavatory - one for big bottoms and one for little ones."

Despite the spartan nature of the average outside lavatory, there were folk to whom it was more than just a refuge in time of need. Many a Norfolk countryman, after a day's toil in the fields, was happy to seek solace within its walls and enjoy half an hour or so with his pipe, the smoke rising upwards and emerging through the ventilation gap at the top of the door as if to announce the election of a new Pope.

And stranger things than that have happened. Ann happily recalls the day when, passing near their two-seater, she heard a voice coming from within. It was at the time when speedway riders like Paddy Mills, Bert Spencer and Billy Bales were thrilling their supporters every week at the Firs Stadium in Norwich. Ann and her brothers were avid speedway fans - especially one brother, and it was his voice that came from within that modest structure and caused her to pause and listen.

"...and now here comes Bert Spencer round the second bend, and he's being caught by Paddy Mills..." and so it went on and on. He was giving an imaginary running commentary on one of the races at the Firs.

"He has never lived it down to this day," says Ann.

That incident, of course, took place in comparatively recent times, but Ann's sister Irene, being so many years older, recalls the times when pony and trap was the main means of travel, and when even a trip to nearby Themelthorpe for the Chapel Anniversary was something of an event. She was very young at the time, but has never forgotten a family who were always there - father, mother and two daughters, glamorous young ladies with long, dangling ear-rings and big picture hats. They came from Jordan, she was told, and she thought they must be very grand to be able to come all that way. Only later did she realise that Jordan was a small parish just a little way down the road.

Irene's aunt was a strictly religious woman and a hard worker for the chapel. Every year, on the day before the Anniversary (always celebrated on the first Sunday in July), she would have a big bowl of the last of the strawberries from the local fruit grower, who also happened to be a local preacher. Straight away, she would 'hull' and sugar them to keep them fresh for the big day.

"I expect they would have kept perfectly well in her cold dairy," says Irene, "but anything that could be done on Saturday had to be done on Saturday in her household. Her husband and sons had to shave before they went to bed on Saturday night. It was, of course, necessary to milk the cows and feed the stock on Sunday," she says, "but the rest of the day was devoted to Chapel - Sunday School in the morning, services afternoon and evening."

On one Sunday, on a visit to their relatives, one of the cousins proudly displayed a wireless set he had made. They were eager to hear it, but he was not allowed to switch it on "in case there was a 'song' on at the time, and 'songs' were absolutely taboo on a Sunday - it was hymns only."

It is probably not surprising that the first book title Irene could read as a child was "Sacred Songs and Solos," which stood permanently on Mother's piano.

The first 'poem' she ever learnt for Sunday School was one which must have echoed through countless churches and chapels over the years:

Jesus bids us smile with a small clear light,
Like a little candle burning in the night.
In this world of darkness, so we must shine,
You in your small corner and I in mine.

By the time we reached this point I felt that my three informants had painted a splendid picture of what growing up in the Norfolk countryside had been like all those years ago. Yet there remained one question I wanted to put to them. Sadly, I was too late in the case of Irene, but the other two responded readily when I asked if there was anything in their lives that, for one reason or another, found a permanent place in their memories.

Ann, perhaps predictably, recalled a domestic situation. It was a day when she was too ill to go to school but, instead of having to stay in bed all day, she was allowed to come down in the afternoon and lie on the couch in front of the fire with a blanket over her. It was a Tuesday - she remembers it well, for Mother was doing the ironing, and Tuesday was always Ironing Day.

"In those days," she said, "we had old-fashioned irons, which consisted of a small block, like a brick, which you heated until it was red hot and then put in a metal container which, when moved, would make a clunking noise. I will never forget the soothing effect it had on me as I lay with my eyes closed just listening to the gentle clunking noise as the iron went back and forth. I was at peace, secure, for Mum was there, doing the ironing."

Jess, very much an outdoor girl, plumped for the lambing season. Mr Ives, the shepherd, had his hut on wheels in the meadow where the ewes were to produce their young, and Jess and her sister would go and help to feed the ones whose mothers had died.

"Mr Ives skinned dead lambs and put the skin on one who had

no mother," she told me, "and the ewe with a dead lamb would smell the skin and think the lamb was hers and let it feed."

Throughout the lambing season Mr Ives slept in his hut, where he had a shelf full of potions for various ailments, as well as a small closed-in stove, for it was often very cold in January and February. There, too, was his dog - "a sort of shabby Dulux dog with long, tangled hair."

"The nice part," said Jess, "was to see the lambs frolic in the meadow. This was the shepherd's harvest time. The more live ewes and lambs he had, the more extra money for him."

Finally, as a kind of postscript, I quote just one more memory each from Ann and Jess. Keeping them until the end was a deliberate act, for I feel they both demonstrate the great love and respect for their parents which was so deeply instilled into children who grew up in the first half of the twentieth century.

First comes Ann, the farmer's daughter, born in time of peace just a few years before the outbreak of the Second World War:

"I don't remember being 'told off' very many times, but I do remember once when I *was* told off by Mother, and that was when she heard me call my brother "a little s∗∗." Where I'd learnt it from I dont know, because I must say that one of the nice things about my childhood was that I never heard Mother or Father swear."

Finally there is Jess, daughter of the village blacksmith, born in the middle of the First World War:

"I remember Dad standing looking out at a lovely downpour of much-needed rain, and he would say 'Thankee, thankee.' I suppose he was talking to the Almighty, although he wasn't a very religious man. He didn't ever swear, but if something went wrong he used a mixture of two swear words and came out with an explosive "Darst!" I still say "Thankee, thankee" when we get a much-wanted rain."

CHAPTER 5

Murder At The Seaside

It was on September 22nd 1900 that the townsfolk of Yarmouth, as well as those of Norfolk and far beyond, were horrified by the news that the dead body of a young woman had been found on the South Beach. She had been strangled with a bootlace pulled tightly round her neck and tied with a reef knot – an unusual knot in those pre-Boy Scout days and not in common use, except among the yachting and fishing fraternities.

The body was examined by the police surgeon, Dr Thomas Lettis, who made a special note of severe injuries that he found. Then began the police investigation, which proved to involve a tangled web of intrigue and mystery that would surely have tested the combined investigative talents of Hercule Poirot and Miss Marple. It took them little short of two months to even establish her real identity and, from that point on, it became a tangle of lies and deceit, confidence trickery and more lies – in fact, almost every form of malpractice known to man.

But the story really begins a week earlier, on the evening of Saturday September 15th. A certain Mrs Rudrum was sitting, quietly ruminating, in the parlour of her modest home at No. 3, Row 104. Like so many other Yarmouth housewives, Mrs Rudrum made a living by accommodating visiting holidaymakers, and she had just seen the departure of the last of her summer guests. Now, like the rest of the town, she was taking a breather before the annual arrival of the fishing fleets in search of their herring harvest.

Suddenly, however, her silent meditation was disturbed by a knock at her front door, and she opened it to reveal a young woman with a suitcase in one hand and a young baby tucked under her other arm. She wanted accommodation, and Mrs Rudrum welcomed her into her home, inwardly pleased at letting a room so late in the season. She certainly had not the slightest inkling of the drama which was later to unfold.

The young woman gave her name as 'Mrs Hood' but said little about herself apart from the fact that she was a widow with a rather splendid house in York and that she had travelled up from London with her brother-in-law, who wanted to marry her. He, she said, was staying at a nearby hotel.

As soon as she had put the baby to bed, Mrs Hood went out to rejoin her companion, arriving back at the lodgings quite late at night, and this was repeated on each day of her stay. Her brother-in-law never came into the house, but he was seen by various members of the Rudrum household as their lodger lingered in the shadows saying goodbye to him.

On the Friday after her arrival in Yarmouth, however, a letter bearing a Woolwich postmark arrived for Mrs Hood. She never mentioned who the letter was from, but she did confide to her landlady that it contained an invitation to meet somebody at 9 o'clock on the following evening under the big clock at the Town Hall.

She spent extra care the next day in preparing herself for her evening assignation. She left her lodgings at about 8-30, and Mrs Rudrum's daughter, Alice, saw her waiting by the Town Hall just before 9 o'clock.

Alice was the last person known to have seen her alive. Her body was found on the South Beach the next morning, strangled by a bootlace.

The police immediately swung into action, but it was a long time before any progress could be made. The trouble was that, throughout her stay in Yarmouth, everything Mrs Hood had told her landlady was found to be nothing more than a tissue of lies. To begin with, she was not a widow, there was no splendid house in York and there was certainly no brother-in-law who wanted to marry her. Even more significantly, the name under which she had taken up her lodgings in Row 104 was false.

The big breakthrough came after seven long and intensive weeks of investigation when it was established that 'Mrs Hood' was, in reality, Mary Jane Bennett, the wife of Herbert John Bennett, a shop assistant.

They had been married in 1897 at Leytonstone Registry Office, but those three years of married life were little more than a tangle of lies and deceit. There were periods of poverty, suddenly relieved by a surge of affluence, invariably acquired by nefarious means. They were, indeed, a disreputable pair.

When Herbert first met Mary he was working as a shop assistant for the Co-op at Northfleet, in Kent, with a weekly wage of just fourteen shillings. Mary, who was blessed with a degree of musical talent, earned a living by teaching the piano and violin in the front parlour of her grandparents' home in the same town.

Strangely enough, Bennett had some sort of interest in music, and he became her pupil. They immediately found that they were soulmates. "Both," it was said, "could lie as easily as they could breathe and could cheat with the smoothness of experienced confidence tricksters."

The lessons continued until the spring of 1897, when Mary found herself pregnant. It was then that Herbert did probably the only decent thing in his entire life – he married her. Even then, however, he found it necessary to lie in order to get the necessary licence. He said that he was 22 and that his parents were dead. The true facts were that he was only 18 and his parents were very much alive.

The early weeks of their married life found them in a state of abject poverty, continually moving from one dingy boarding house to another in and around London. Suddenly, however, their financial situation took a dramatic turn for the better, and they achieved a state of affluence sufficient to enable them to move into a comfortable flat in Wandsworth.

Not surprisingly, the sudden change in their fortunes was brought about by a confidence trick, cunningly conceived and carried out. Mary put an advertisement in *Exchange and Mart,* couched in the following terms:

Poor widow woman has precious old violin for sale, worth £100 – will accept £1 if immediate.

Orders flooded in, and the pair were kept busy with deliveries, for it was not just a single violin they had to offer, nor was it either precious or old. They had, in fact, found a source from which they could obtain cheap, trashy instruments for around £1 a dozen.

By September 1899 they had acquired sufficient capital for a legitimate business, and they moved to Balham and set up as greengrocers. Early the following year the Bennetts sold the business and bought a grocery shop at Westgate-on-Sea for £535.

Little more than a week later, the shop was completely destroyed by fire and, suspecting nothing, the insurance company paid out a handsome settlement. The Bennetts immediately rented the shop next door, acquired a large quantity of goods on credit and, after a few weeks trading, simply disappeared, with their creditors setting up a hue and cry for their money. Before the full nature of the fraud was realised, however, the Bennetts were well out of range, on their way to South Africa – travelling as 'Mr and Mrs Hood.'

By May they were back in England and, the following month, they came to the mutual decision that it would be best if their marriage came to an end. They gave no thought to divorce, and the parting was completely amicable on both sides. They went their separate ways, but they still remained friends.

Herbert Bennett proceeded to take up regular employment at Woolwich Arsenal, and it was while he was working there that he met a parlour maid named Alice Meadows. Alice was a pretty girl of 22, rather serious but good-natured, and Bennett fell desperately in love with her.

During the August Bank Holiday week they took a holiday together. Bennett was very keen to go to Ireland, but he gave in to Alice's wish for Yarmouth, where they stayed at what was then the Crown and Anchor Hotel. Herbert seemed to have no shortage of money, and they both enjoyed their week together. They returned to London on August 6th and, within a few days, Alice had accepted his proposal of marriage.

All the while, however, the net was closing in on him and, when the detectives began unravelling the web of 'Mrs Hood's' strange life, they felt they had got their man. After all, he had the motive – he had fallen in love with another woman and wanted to marry her. And he was unable – or, perhaps, unwilling – to produce an alibi.

Herbert Bennett was eventually arrested on November 5th, prior to which he had behaved in a perfectly normal manner and continued to work at Woolwich Arsenal. He protested his innocence right from the start, though a large swell of public opinion believed him to be guilty even before the trial started.

His defence barrister, Edward Marshall Hall – described as 'one of the greatest advocates of all time' – was totally convinced of his client's innocence. Then, long before the end of the trial, there was a great shift in public opinion towards the belief that, though damned by his notorious past, he was not guilty of this particular crime.

The trouble was that nobody, apart from Bennett himself, knew anything about his movements on the day and night of the murder, September 22nd. The landlady at his lodgings saw him that morning studying a railway time-table and saying that he had a train to catch. Evidence was given that his bed was not slept in that night. Grounds for suspicion, perhaps, but surely not evidence of guilt.

Furthermore, when he left his lodgings that morning he was wearing a smart, light grey suit and a bowler hat. When he met Alice in Hyde Park the next morning he was still wearing the same clothes. If he had killed Mary he certainly must have had a change of clothing somewhere, for the police surgeon had said that she had been savagely attacked and that the perpetrator must have left the scene with heavy bloodstains about his person. But Herbert had carried no case when he left Woolwich, and no blood-stained clothing had ever been found.

It seems strange that Herbert Bennett, competent liar that he was, had made no effort to concoct an alibi to cover his movements on that fateful day. Could it have been that his belief in his own innocence would carry him through? Or was there some other reason?

It was then that a bombshell was dropped on the proceedings with evidence that Bennett had certain contacts with Ireland at that time, and the accusation was made that he had been stealing weapons from the Arsenal and selling them to the I.R.A. This would account for his occasional disappearances and would certainly explain his state of affluence.

Herbert protested his innocence throughout, and Marshall Hall "fought like a tiger" to save him, but all to no avail. He was found guilty of murder and sentenced to death by hanging.

But who was the man Mary was meeting during her stay in Yarmouth? It was certainly not Herbert for, at the time when she was seen lingering and kissing in the shadows, there were a host of people ready to swear he was in Woolwich. And there was certainly no brother-in-law.

It was a bitterly cold, grey morning when Herbert Bennett was executed at Norwich Prison at 9 o'clock on March 21st 1901. A silent crowd had gathered outside, mostly holding the belief that an innocent man was being sent to his death. He had been condemned, they believed, on the evidence of his past life rather than of the charge that had been made against him in the courtroom.

The execution was carried out, and then, in accordance with custom, a black flag was raised from the flagstaff above the prison.

Then, to the accompaniment of a massive gasp from the crowd, the pole cracked, bringing the mast and flag clattering down in the prison yard. It was an omen, they said – sure proof of Herbert Bennett's innocence.

It was a strange happening that remained for a long time a subject for discussion and conjecture. Gradually, however, with the passage of the years, it was to fade in the memories of the people of Yarmouth. But it was not the end of the story – far from it.

Eleven years later, on July 14th 1912, the body of another young woman was found on the South Beach. She was 18-year-old Dora May Gray, and it proved to be a complete carbon copy of the murder of Mary Jane Bennett.

Every detail was identical. She had been strangled with a bootlace tied tightly round her neck with a reef knot, and she was found in exactly the same position on the beach. Furthermore, injuries had been inflicted on her body which were an exact replica of those found on the previous body. The examination of the body was carried out by the same police surgeon, Dr Thomas Lettis, who had no hesitation in declaring that both murders must have been committed by the same hand.

"The details of both crimes," he said, "are so similar that it is far beyond the realms of possibility that the second murder is merely a case of one murderer imitating the methods of another."

In both cases there was a mysterious man who was never identified. In the case of Mary Jane Bennett he was described as a tall dark man with a moustache. He was said to be a yachtsman *aged about 30,* and his first name was thought to be Percy.

In the enquiry into the second murder, witnesses told the police that Dora May Gray had been keeping company with a tall dark man with a moustache. He, too, was a yachtsman *aged about 40* and his name was Percy.

The killer of Dora May Gray was never found, but the second murder would seem to vindicate Herbert Bennett in his plea of innocence in the case concerning Mary Jane. Certainly he could not have murdered Dora May Gray, for Death had given him the perfect alibi.

2

These We Have Loved

CHAPTER 6

Ted Ellis of Wheatfen

The scene was a village churchyard a few miles east of Norwich, very close to the edge of Broadland. It had been the most splendid of summer days, with the sun shining down from a sky as blue as a dunnock's egg to feed the earth below with life-giving warmth. Now, it was early evening, but still that same aura of warmth pervaded the land, and it seemed that all nature was alive and going about its business.

There were just two token signs of human life in God's Acre that evening – first, a man seated on the grass between the rows of ancient headstones, his head tilted to one side and his hand cupped against his ear, silently listening; then the voices of the village choir, blending in mellow unison and wafting out on the balmy summer air as they practised next Sunday's hymns.

Then, a third human presence came on the scene in the form of another man who, seeing the seated figure on the grass, started to walk towards him. The sound of the choir fell softly on his ears as he made his approach, and then, as if neither wished to break the magic of the moment, the two men each raised a hand in mutual recognition. The new arrival paused for a brief moment and then, as the sound of the voices faded, he spoke.

"What a delightful sound," he said.

"Yes," said the seated listener, his hand still cupped against his ear. "And the amazing thing is that they do it by rubbing their back legs together."

It was not the sound of the choir that had captured his rapt attention. He had been listening to the grasshoppers carrying on a conversation under the cover of the grass which was their home.

This is a true story – nothing fictional about it. In fact, the seated listener was Ted Ellis and the second man was me. I must hasten to add that both Ted and I were well aware that a grasshopper does *not* rub its legs together for the purpose of communication – it has a horny patch on its forewing for that specific function. His reversion to an earlier childhood fallacy was just an example of the puckish sense of humour which made a conversation with him so pleasurable.

Ted Ellis was Norfolk's favourite countryman, a self-taught naturalist with an ever-observant eye and a constant urge to communicate his findings to anybody who chose to listen.

"Ted," said one who knew him, "was rather like a bittern, a creature that lives – skulks, even – in the reedbeds, with a lovely mischievous twinkle in his eye."

He walked through our countryside and wrote about it with such insight and originality as to put him high among the ranks of our best country writers – and beside him, and always part of it all, was his wife Phyllis.

Ted was not a Norfolk man by birth, having entered this world on the Island of Guernsey in 1909, but he was soon destined to become more part of the Norfolk scene than many of its natives. His parents – mother was a teacher and father a singer – had been convinced by their life on the Island during the Great War that their family aspirations would be better served by moving to the mainland. Hence, back they came to their family roots on the East Anglian coast to set up home in Gorleston.

Once there, Ted threw himself into his study of the world of nature and, even at the age of twelve, he was keeping a record of everything he saw and heard. He talked to the people of the countryside – farm workers and smallholders, reed cutters and thatchers – and everything went into his copious notebooks, together with his own drawings of what he saw.

One day, with his younger brother Martin, he cycled to Yarmouth to introduce himself to A.H. Patterson, that outstanding man of Breydon who, under the pseudonym of John Knowlittle, had become a legend with his copious writings about natural life. There began an immediate friendship between the two naturalists – the old man and the beginner – and Patterson was not slow to recognise the precocious talent of the young teenager.

"Young Ellis," he wrote, "hath the eyes of a falcon and the optimism of a Sancho Panza."

During the remainder of his schooldays Ted spent all his free time either observing nature or writing about it, and it was this latter talent that began to attract a wider following. At the age of sixteen, his nature notes were appearing in the parish magazine, and gradually they began to find their way into the pages of the local Press. His was a deceptively simple style, but the pieces he wrote were not mere recordings of biological facts. He had the eye of a naturalist and the soul of a poet. His writings had a sense of rhythm and a descriptive quality which broadened their appeal to a wider audience than simply nature lovers:

I walked along the shore of Breydon Water from Yarmouth to Burgh Castle. The day was clear and sunny with little wind, and the tide was rising, gradually spreading over the mudflats and precipitating restless movements among the wading birds, especially dunlins – thousands, bunched in twisting and turning flocks, flashed like swirling snowflakes at one moment and darkly receded from view a moment later as they rose and dived at speed, whistling as they passed.

Ted made his first public appearance as a speaker on November 16th, 1927. It was at Arnolds Restaurant in Yarmouth, where he addressed members of the Rotary Club on the subject of "Some Delights of a Young Naturalist." It was before the days of slide projectors, but his talk was well illustrated with his own detailed drawings, produced on the back of sheets of wallpaper.

He joined Yarmouth Naturalists' Society, became its Secretary and, on occasions when a speaker was not available, he was ever eager, at a moment's notice, to fill the breach. I think it could be said that Fate played a part in his joining the Society, for it was there that he first met Phyllis. She was a member and a regular attender at meetings, though it was to be some time before romance was to blossom. On one occasion, his mother insisted that he went to a local dance, and he grudgingly obeyed. Phyllis was there and, during the course of the evening, seeing him sitting miserably alone, she went across to talk to him. She asked if he would like to dance with her.

"I don't think I know how to," came the reply.

But they did manage to get round the floor – "after a fashion," said Phyllis.

Then came the day when Ted's father decided it was time for his son to take up full-time employment but, of course, there was not much scope for professional naturalists in those days. As luck would have it, however, his old friend Arthur Patterson was then living at Hellesdon, and he knew there was a vacancy at a private zoo at Keswick Hall, just outside Norwich. The owner, Gerard Gurney, needed a new helper, and thus it was that Ted Ellis took up his employment as Keeper of Foreign Birds.

I have a feeling that the position was not entirely to his liking, for he preferred the creatures of the Norfolk countryside to caged

Ted Ellis in his teenage years at Keswick Hall, 1927.

birds from foreign climes. It did, however, provide him with a steady income while he increased his stock of material for both articles and lectures, for which there was a steadily increasing demand. By July 1927, however, the call of the open country became too strong to be denied and, leaving Keswick, he resumed his friendship with Arthur Patterson, who had, by then, returned to his old Breydon haunts.

There, the two naturalists, one elderly and the other still a teenager, rambled through the countryside together and shared their mutual devotion to everything they saw around them. It was during this period that Ted typed the manuscript of the older man's latest work, *Wildfowlers and Poachers,* a book now long out of print and very much a collector's item.

The following year, after twelve carefree months of free-range wandering and writing, something was to happen which would mark a turning point in the young man's life. The Castle Museum in Norwich was entering a new era, and the decision was made to appoint a Curator of Natural History to take the place into the future. The position was advertised, and it is no secret that a number of people in influential positions took steps to make sure Ted saw it. Urged on by many of his admirers, he applied and duly attended for interview. Being entirely self-taught, he had no formal qualifications to offer, so he took his natural history notebooks and they helped him to clinch the matter. It was the wisest decision the Museum trustees could possibly have made.

It was in November 1928 that he took up his new position and, within a year, a chance meeting with a visitor to the Museum led to his finding the cottage where, in due course, he and Phyllis would spend forty years together. The visitor was Captain Maurice Cockle who, in the course of conversation, told Ted that he had bought a nice little estate – a hundred acres and a marshman's cottage – where he was living in retirement. It was called *Wheatfen* and he invited Ted to visit him there.

Needless to say, Ted accepted the invitation, and he was absolutely fascinated by the place. With such a wealth of different habitats, it was a naturalist's delight. Rich in bird life, there was woodland, then the fens and a whole chain of little waterways left by the peat diggings of mediaeval times.

Ted paid many visits to *Wheatfen* and did systematic surveys there from 1929 and through the 1930s, by which time he must surely have known the place better than any other in the county.

In 1936 he took Phyllis to see it. They cycled the 22 miles from Gorleston and then went on the Broad in the marshman's boat. Phyllis marvelled at the sparkle and clarity of the water, clearly revealing the fish, the water plants and, deep below, the mussels on the very bottom. She thought how nice it would be to live there, but they had to wait until after the Second World War before their dreams were realised.

In November 1945 Captain Cockle died, and his widow, not wanting to stay there alone, decided to move near relatives in Margate. She offered Ted and Phyllis the chance to hire the place, and they duly moved in at the end of the following January. It was not exactly a world of luxury. There was no electricity, water came in a bucket from the well, and there was just wood for fires, but Ted was in his element. He had no need to go looking for nature – he just had to open the door and it came to him!

He was now in the happy position where the Museum was providing his income and the framework for his research, whilst all his free time was channelled into his writing. But the sheer enthusiasm and passion which had shone through his observations brought forth a strong feeling of empathy from his readers, and the demand for more was ever-increasing.

He produced his first book, a standard work on the natural history of the Broads, in the 1950s; then came a fortnightly column for the *Guardian* in the 1960s, and then there followed his blossoming relationship with BBC radio and television, which brought him even wider recognition. And all the while there was his daily column in the *Eastern Daily Press,* a mammoth commitment which he carried out for so many years. This had to be in the editor's hands by 10pm on the previous evening and, though he had an inclination to leave things until the last minute, he never let them down.

Sometimes a letter or specimen from a reader would get him going. Then it might be a simple topic like an autumn morning which would arouse the poet in him, with words like these:

Sunshine over the Fen on these autumn mornings brings transient splendour to a realm of dew-wet reeds and the lingering cloak of mist. Through a haze of rose which turns to gold, countless geometric webs of spiders bridge darkening gaps, glittering and opalescent. Spear leaves and drooping purple reed blooms are beaded with silver and the pincushion umbles of angelica are pricked out with a million diamond points of light.

On other occasions, fellow naturalists would come up with something – men like Ken Durrant, the insect man of Beeston Common – another self-taught student of nature, and with the most delightful of Norfolk accents to boot!

I still cherish the memory of an occasion when I was able to bring to Ted's notice a species which he had not previously encountered.

I had gone to Burnham Deepdale to photograph the splendid font which stood just inside the church. It was, indeed, the church's greatest treasure, a Norman creation carved from a solid block of stone, with one side adorned with trees and foliage, and the other three depicting scenes, month by month, throughout the year. It was also a famous font, known far and wide to all who study English churches, and it was further renowned, almost unbelievably, for having served for almost forty years of its life, as a cistern at Fincham rectory.

I was in a state of great anticipation as I arrived at Deepdale, never expecting anything to distract me from my mission. Yet, this is just what happened. As I put my hand on the churchyard gate, my eyes happened to light on a cluster of flowers on both the side and, in even greater splendour, on the top of the adjoining wall. At first glance they had the appearance of mere daisies, but there was something about them that made them different, and I recalled something I had read about a related species, originating in Mexico, which had been seen just once in this country – on the south coast of the Isle of Wight. It was believed that seeds must have made their way there on one of the many ships which passed through those waters. All thoughts of the font went from my mind as I made my way home to consult my book and look at the photograph of this new arrival.

Having done that, I felt even more sure about the plant, but there was only one way to be completely certain. I rang Ted and described my discovery to him and, as luck would have it, he was due to give a talk in the neighbourhood of Deepdale a few days later, so he would go and see for himself. A few days later, he telephoned me and, with almost boyish glee, confirmed that what I had found really was what I thought it to be. A few more days passed, and then the icing really was on the cake when, in his column in the *EDP*, he told his readers of the discovery in Norfolk of *Mexican Fleabane*.

Ted had given up his post at the Museum in 1956 after 28 years as Curator and was then able to dedicate himself to full-time writing, but it was still not an easy task. Furthermore, as the years went by, both he and Phyllis became aware of something which was of much greater concern to them. The Broads were gradually dying. The question of nature conservation had been overlooked in the face of growing pressure to throw the Broads open to all who wished to visit them. In their earlier days at *Wheatfen*, the only thing which passed across their skyline was the sail of an occasional wherry. Now, Phyllis recalls the day when she took a boat out on Surlingham Broad and found the entire surface of the water covered by a skin of diesel from the exhausts of the ever-increasing number of pleasure boats that passed that way.

Then there was the degradation which resulted from modern intensive farming practices, with the consequent poisoning of the surrounding land with agro-chemicals, not to mention the pressure from the building of new houses for people who wanted to live there.

The waters, once so crystal clear, became dark and dirty. The fish were gone; *Wheatfen's* kingfishers disappeared. The publishers of Ted's earlier book put pressure on him to republish, but he declined. The book had become outdated – he said that he would have needed to re-write everything in it.

There are many who felt that the Broads should have been declared a National Park decades ago – Julian Huxley called for it in the 1940s – but nothing was done until 1986, when a meeting took place in London to establish a Broads Authority. Its purpose was to try and strike a balance between the demands made on the area by the different interested parties.

When that meeting took place, Ted was already a dying man, but somehow he managed to rouse himself to go to London and put forth his views on the future of Broadland.

The writing carried on until the end:

For the past week, my view of Norfolk has been restricted to what can be seen from a hospital bed in Norwich. Mostly I have to be content with the sky itself.....

Ted will not see the restoration of *Wheatfen* to its former glory but, somehow, he will always be there. In the words of David Bellamy:

"When you now walk the Fen, you can still feel the image of Ted, the very spirit of Ted."

CHAPTER 7

The Bellman's Grandson

It has always been my belief that Fate decreed that Alf Harvey should become Wymondham's 'man of the people.' After all, he had the pedigree for it. To begin with, in the early years after his birth in 1910, he came very much under the influence of his grandfather, Jesse Harvey.

Jesse, a formidable figure, was Wymondham's bellman, or town crier, trudging the streets of the town and making announcements for people who sought publicity for their activities. Organisers of concerts and sporting events, as well as local tradesmen, sought his help to publicise what they had to offer – all for a fee of a shilling for twenty 'calls.'

Then there were the nationally renowned Annual Sports Days organised by Wymondham Athletic Club. Thousands of spectators would gather on the King's Head Meadow, with special rail excursions running from all over the county and many competitors coming from much further afield. Ever present, too, was Jesse Harvey, complete with bell, shouting "Competitors for the One Mile Race, come out!" and then announcing the winners.

Jesse died in 1914, to be followed as bellman by his son, also named Jesse. He filled the post for thirty years until, in 1945, advances in public communication had made it something of an anachronism, and he duly handed in the bell. One can only wonder whether, if society had not seen such advances, young Alf would have become the third Harvey bellman.

Long before that, however, Alf had left school and, finding great difficulty in obtaining employment, had eventually been taken on by a printing company in Oxford. He was not particularly happy with the situation but, after a few years, the hand of Fate played another card, in a most unfortunate manner. He was involved in some kind of accident, as the result of which he lost the thumb from his left hand. In a strange way, however, it was a blessing in disguise for, nothing daunted, Alf came back to Wymondham, married his sweetheart Gertie and opened a fish and chip shop in Damgate Street.

Alf was a fun man and, before long, he adorned his shop front with the slogan 'Alf's is the pla(i)ce for fish.' Fortunately his customers agreed with him, and business flourished. Before long, he acquired a van and began a mobile fish and chip service, firstly in the shadow of the Market Cross and later to a number of surrounding villages, where potential customers would always be awaiting his arrival.

But not all his ventures met with that degree of success. There was an occasion, not long before the outbreak of the Second World War, when the Labour Party were due to hold a massive rally in Wymondham. The number of people attending was so large that it was decided that the only venue big enough was the King's Head Meadow.

Scenting the smell of business, Alf was like a man inspired. The day before the rally, he went in his van to Norwich Fish Market, where he proceeded to fill the vehicle with as many sacks of cockles as it would hold. Then it was back to Wymondham, where he and Gertie worked long into the night boiling the cockles and preparing bottles of vinegar and little dishes in which to serve their delicacy.

Came the day – and came the monsoon! The heavens opened and continuous torrential rain fell. The King's Head Meadow was flooded to such an extent that the proceedings had to be switched to the Regal Cinema.

At that point, a lesser man would have thrown in the towel, but not Alf. That evening, he and Gertie loaded up the van and set off on a tour of all the public houses in the district – and there were many! The drinkers welcomed them, and some of the publicans even suggested they should make it a weekly routine. But Alf declined – once was quite enough.

Then came the war and, like so many other young men, Alf was determined to join the forces and 'do his bit.' In September 1940 he achieved his ambition by joining the Royal Artillery, although one cannot help wondering whether a one-thumbed gunner might have been at a disadvantage in the heat of battle. His satisfaction at donning military uniform was, however, short-lived for, just a few months later, he was discharged on medical grounds (could it have been that thumb?) and returned to civilian life.

He was utterly devastated, but he was never a man to accept defeat readily, and soon he realised that there were other ways to help the war effort. Hence, he hit upon the idea of hiring a barrel organ and playing it around the town whenever there was a money-making event like War Weapons Week, Warships Week or Wings For Victory.

It was during this period that he evolved the idea of putting himself into character while playing the barrel organ. He thought long and hard and eventually came up with the idea of being a Pearly King. It was a decision that was to bring him widespread recognition, not just in Norfolk but also in many other parts of the country.

Alf and Gertie were a splendid team and, as soon as he told her of his ambition, she set to work to make the long-tailed coat, the trousers and the floppy peaked cap in the appropriate style. Then came the arduous task of sewing on literally hundreds of pearly white buttons which completed the transformation.

Having completed the task, it was then Gertie's turn to make a decision. If Alf was to be the town's Pearly King, then she would be his Pearly Queen. Hence, she set to work to produce a costume for herself. The result was dramatic, and the pair, with barrel organ, became a regular feature in every carnival procession and at every fete or other charity event that took place in the area. There can be little doubt that most people who still remember Alf and Gertie carry in their minds a vision of the Pearly King and Queen of Wymondham.

By this time, incidentally, Alf had stumbled upon an old barrel organ, long cast aside and serving as a roosting place for chickens in the back yard of a public house. He bought the instrument for £1 and, in spite of his limited knowledge of its inner workings, succeeded in restoring it to its former glory. He glowed with pride at being the owner of the organ, with the added convenience of no longer having to hire one for each event.

Although Alf and Gertie worked together in such a splendid partnership, there was one day in the week when, during the winter months, they went their separate ways. The reason was that Alf was an avid football fan and a dedicated supporter of Norwich City. Whether it was a home match at Carrow Road or an away encounter at some faraway place anywhere else in the country, he would leave Gertie in charge of the shop and join a group of friends on their weekly mission.

It seems inevitable that, on those occasions, he should don his Pearly King outfit, though with certain modifications. Firstly, the multitude of buttons, hitherto pristinely pearly white, were painted

Alf Harvey, organ grinder.

yellow and green, and then he adopted a new prop in the form of a long pole, from the end of which hung a birdcage containing a toy canary. Thus adorned, he became the unofficial Norwich City mascot, parading around the pitch and whipping up the enthusiasm of the Canary supporters.

He made his first appearance in his new guise in 1954, when the Canaries went to Highbury to cross swords with the mighty Arsenal in the fourth round of the F.A. Cup. He was warmly received by both sets of supporters but, at the end of the match, Alf and his mates were the happy ones, for lowly Norwich had beaten their illustrious opponents by two goals to one.

Throughout his long career as Canary mascot, there was only one occasion when he encountered opposition to his antics, and that only arose as a result of his over-enthusiasm. It was during Norwich City's illustrious F.A. Cup run in the 1958-59 season, on the day of the fifth round, when they travelled to White Hart Lane to play the formidable Tottenham Hotspurs. The Canary supporters arrived at the ground long before the match, and Alf was in the middle of his efforts to rouse their enthusiasm when on to the

Alf Harvey, Canaries supporter – complete with sleeveless fur coat.

pitch marched a military band to provide some pre-match entertainment. Without a moment's hesitation, Alf darted across to the band with the idea of helping to conduct them. The supporters cheered, but it was all too much for three members of the local constabulary, who stopped him in his tracks and removed him from the hallowed turf, to the accompaniment of a large outburst of booing and whistling from the supporters.

Apart from that one incident, Alf unfailingly received a warm welcome from both groups of supporters at every ground he visited. Indeed, he proudly boasted that, in all his career, the only missile that ever hit him was a miniature chocolate Swiss roll. In time, he became something of a nationwide celebrity, with national newspapers and television reporting his exuberant weekly antics.

One other story of Alf's footballing career is worth recalling. It was a bitterly cold January morning in 1956 when he and his colleagues made their way down to the railway station to start a journey to Sunderland. There had been a hard frost in the night and, with an icy wind blowing, the temperature was destined to stay below freezing point all day. Gertie was busy in the shop and, as English people do, she began discussing the cold weather with a woman customer.

"But," said the woman, "I saw your Alf and his mates by the station this morning, and he looked nice and snug in his fur coat."

Gertie was puzzled, for Alf did not have a fur coat. But, as she always said, she "would never be surprised at anything Alf would do." No doubt he had picked it up at some jumble sale.

She thought no more about it and, at the end of the day, she locked up the shop and made her way home. It was then that all was revealed. It was her fur coat that he had taken and, in order to get his arms in, he had removed the sleeves and left them behind!

Eventually, Alf gave up frying fish and chips and switched to wet fish on one side of his shop and greengrocery on the other. Then, some years later, with his daughter Sheila to help him, he concentrated solely on greengrocery, and he became a familiar figure, in the small hours of the morning, visiting Norwich Wholesale Market to get the best fruit and vegetables.

Alf was 75 when he died in 1985, but by that time he had become more than just a Wymondham character. He was a man of the people, and now he is a figure of local folklore. Those of us who knew him still miss seeing him about the place.

CHAPTER 8

At The Going Down Of The Sun

For more than eighty years we have steadfastly commemorated Armistice Day. It is true that the hurly burly and motorised mayhem of modern society has made it necessary to switch the main happenings to the nearest Sunday, but we still mark both dates in our various fashions.

One pleasing trend in recent years is the apparent increase of young people assembling in church or round the war memorial, yet I often wonder what those youthful onlookers are thinking as the banners unfurl, the bugle sounds and silence falls on the congregation.

What, indeed, were the thoughts that went through my mind all those years ago when, as a young lad, I paraded in the Market Place with the 1st North Walsham Wolf Cubs? We knew it to be a very special day, one of the most important in the rural calendar, when we must remember the men who died so that we could be free. But, how could we remember them when we had never known them?

Rural happenings on Armistice Day were always impressive because of their very simplicity. Schoolchildren were there, many in the guise of Scouts, Guides and Brownies. There was just a short service, sometimes with the help of the Salvation Army Band; wreaths were laid at the foot of the memorial; and then came the two minutes silence, religiously observed. The countryside was mercifully free of motor vehicles in those days, and none came near. If a horse-drawn vehicle came by as the hour of eleven approached, the driver would dismount, bare his head and stand silently by his horse.

Observing the two minutes silence in the countryside was more difficult than in the town, for it was not possible to shut down a farm like a shop, an office or a factory. Long before 11 o'clock the shepherd, the woodman and most of the farm workers were busy about their labours, spread widely over different parts of the land. They overcame this, however, by setting their watches by the church clock when their day began at first light. Then, without the sound of a bugle call, work ceased at the appointed time.

Somehow, I always think that for one man to observe the two minutes silence in total isolation is almost more impressive than when a huge crowd does so. A ploughing team motionless in the middle of a furrow, with the ploughman standing at attention between the plough handles, perhaps thinking back to those dark days when he wondered whether he would ever see his homeland again. A silent, motionless shepherd alone with his flock in the middle of a root field. An elderly woodman standing in a clearing with a billhook in his hand.

A. G. Street, the renowned Wiltshire farmer, writer and broadcaster, recalled the occasion when he saw a local Hunt meet outside a village church and pay homage to Armistice Day.

"Never shall I forget that," he wrote. "A grey Saxon church, a white-haired rector, some surpliced choirboys, and thirty or forty riders in pink and black sitting motionless on their horses. Even the hounds seemed to understand that this was a special occasion. They clustered round the huntsman's horse, looking up anxiously into his face with their tongues lolling out, and during that two minutes forgot even to wag their sterns. Such a meet brings the heaviest Cap of the season, destined, of course, for Earl Haig's fund."

But all that was after the Great War, and I had known nothing of that conflict. My parents had, very considerately, delayed my arrival into the world until several years after the end of hostilities, and nobody who has not personally experienced war can have any understanding of its horrors.

Yet there was evidence of those four years all around us. On almost every street corner there would be a wreck of a man, medals on his chest, begging for help and trying to eke out a living by selling matches or bootlaces. Many carried visible signs of their war service – an empty sleeve or a missing leg with just a crutch to replace it.

And there were other signs. I still remember the day when my mother and I were walking hand-in-hand down Hall Lane to the Council School. Walking ahead of us was a round-shouldered man who suddenly stopped and, turning towards the road, spat into the gutter. We had been taught that spitting in the street was a disgusting habit, so I looked up at my mother's face and said, "He was naughty to do that, wasn't he?" My mother looked down and softly replied, "We must forgive him – he was gassed in the War."

I had no idea what being 'gassed in the War' meant, but I always felt sorry when I saw other men engage in the same habit.

But hostility towards the beaten enemy lingered long in the hearts of the British people, and some of it overflowed into the minds of the children. Germany quickly acquired the art of producing the most splendid tin-plate toys – trains, cars and the like – and they found their way into the local toyshops. Soon we were receiving them as birthday and Christmas presents and, though we knew the country of origin, we welcomed them, for they were splendidly made. But there was always a tinge of hostility, for all German products at that time bore the imprint 'D.R.G.M.' – and we all knew that those little initials stood for 'Dirty Rotten German Make.'

Slowly, however, the hostility began to fade and we, the children of the coming generation, set about the serious business of growing up.

At that time, in North Walsham, there was a group of four lads who became almost inseparable friends. They loved the countryside around them, they thrilled at the flickering black-and-white films at the Picturedome and, every Tuesday, they donned their green jerseys and caps for the weekly Cub Night.

That sprightly quartet consisted of my brother Peter and me, and two other brothers, Kenneth and Douglas Brown. Peter and Kenneth (usually known, for reasons which escape me, as 'Count Brown') were of the same age, whilst Douglas and I were two years younger, and it is worthy of mention that our respective mothers were also on the friendliest of terms. We did not regard ourselves as a 'gang' or anything of that nature. Perhaps we were not always saints, but nor were we sinners. No doubt there was the occasional scrumped apple, the sudden urge to knock on somebody's front door and scamper away to hide behind a bush and watch the outcome – and it was in the Churchyard that we engaged in our gambling activities. However, as the means of our gambling was a set of fivestones and the bets we laid were in the form of cigarette cards, I don't really think we caused harm to anybody.

The great strength of our friendship stemmed from the two older boys, for they were the sort of people who could brighten up the dreariest of days just by being there. The kind who would have been described as 'a damn fine chap' or, in present-day parlance, 'Mister Nice Guy.'

They continued their lives in the same manner when we progressed to Grammar School, and a contemporary of mine was moved to write of them, and two other prefects, with these words: "In those days, to small fry like myself, it was as if the gods walked the earth in the guise of those four."

By 1936 we had all left Paston and gone our various ways. Already, however, war clouds were gathering over Europe. The words of Thomas Gray spring to mind:

'Unmindful of the coming doom
The little victims play.....'

Then came the war, and we became even more widely spread. Peter went with the B.E.F. to France, escaped in the miracle of Dunkirk and, after chasing Rommel backwards and forwards through Benghazi and Tobruk, slowly returned through Europe. Kenneth Brown joined the Norfolks and, like so many local lads, found himself in the living hell of Burma. As for me – I joined the Navy, and perhaps I may be permitted one little memory of the day I left home on my way to Devonport Dockyard.

I was standing in the hallway of our house with my parents and was just about to put my hand on the door handle when my father did something completely out of character. He was proud of his four sons, but he never allowed himself to display any hint of his innermost emotions. At that moment, however, he put his arm around my shoulders and gave me just the slightest of hugs. Then he spoke, very quietly.

"Take care of yourself," he said. "We don't want any dead heroes."

Eventually, after all those seemingly endless years, it was all over, and the lucky ones among us set about the task of getting accustomed to civilian life. It was then that I received a book listing the names of all the Old Boys of Paston who had gone to war but had not come back. It hit me like the blade of a dagger, for there were no less than 67 names on that list, more than forty of which were contemporaries of mine – boys with whom I had worked and played, had taken part in our regular mid-morning P.T. sessions in the Yard – and had spent so many long hours digging plantains from the School Field.

As I read through the list, I pictured each one as I had known him in boyhood. The truth is that they were little more than boys when they lost their lives – some in their early twenties and others still just teenagers.

Then, as I read on, I received possibly the cruellest blow of all as I read:

'Kenneth Brown.....Sgt., Norfolk Regiment.'

Ken had died at Kohima in March 1943, shot in the chest by a sniper's bullet when the 2nd Division were making their stand there.

In due course, his mother received letters from two of his officers, which I was later privileged to read. The first was from his Commanding Officer and must surely have been just one of the vast number that he found it his duty to write at that particular time. It read:

I have known your son ever since he joined us and I can honestly say that I have always regarded him as one of the best of my British N.C.O.s. He was always willing to do a job of work and he was always cheerful. It is not easy to be cheerful in some of the places in which we have been lately, and your son's general behaviour and outlook on life has been an inspiration to both British and African ranks in this unit. He is a great loss to us and I ask you to get what little comfort you can in the knowledge that he died as a good soldier should – in action against the enemy. In this particular battle we hit the beastly Japanese quite a hard crack, due to the fact that people like your son were prepared to give their lives for their country and their comrades.

I know not whether Mrs Brown's grief was relieved by being told that Ken had 'died as a good soldier should – in action against the enemy.' I know full well, however, what my own mother's reactions would have been if that statement had been made concerning one of her sons.

The second letter, nevertheless, was couched in somewhat different terms. It came from Ken's platoon commander and the feelings expressed were those of a friend rather than just a fellow soldier:

We were attacked in camp by a strong party of Japs and our platoon was detailed to put in a counter-attack to cut off the enemy's rear. This we did, but soon became pinned down by heavy fire all around us and it became quite obvious that we should have to soon get out or be surrounded. However, these things cannot be done without orders from a higher source, and your son volunteered to go back to find our company commander.

He did not return, and when we eventually withdrew we found him lying on the jungle path shot through the right breast by a

sniper. We buried him by the banks of the Bun River, in a quiet
little glade of trees.

He and I had a great deal in common, both of us coming from
the country and liking the same good things of life – the birds,
trees, country folk, etc., and many is the chat we had about places
we'd both been to. I'll never forget his cheerful disposition, always
singing or doing some little job to keep himself amused. The black
men loved him and he was a great inspiration and help to me at
all times.

One thing emerges crystal clear from those words. Kenneth
Brown died as he had always lived – a real 'Mister Nice Guy.' I
thank God for the privilege of knowing him – and all those other
young lads at Paston who, at the end of term, belted out with full
gusto the words of the final hymn,

'Lord dismiss us with thy blessing,
Thanks for mercies past received,'
and then, at the first assembly of the next term, with a distinctly
more sotto voce rendition of
'Lord *receive* us with your blessing.'

Every year, on Armistice Day, we remember our promise:
'At the going down of the sun, and in the morning,
We will remember them.'
Then, when we observe the two minutes silence, it is the images
of those boys that fill my mind, together with the words of my
boyhood idol, Rupert Brooke, himself a victim of the First World
War:
If I should die, think only this of me:
That there's some corner of a foreign field
That is for ever England.

68

CHAPTER 9

Lots Were Dressed By Littles

It is doubtful whether many of the shoppers who, in their thousands, daily trudge the pavements of St. Stephen's and The Walk are aware of the fact that, for much of the twentieth century, the main shopping centre of Norwich was elsewhere, almost on the opposite side of the city. That distinction belonged to Magdalen Street and St. Benedict's which, between them, could boast of no fewer than 160 retail outlets.

It was in the glorious age of local family-owned businesses, packed tightly along the length of both streets. There were a few representatives of national concerns such as Boots the Chemist, Brenner's Bazaar and Stead and Simpson's; the grocery trade was represented by small branches of Lipton's, Home & Colonial and the Maypole; and there were one or two Banks - not to mention a splendid selection of public houses. Mostly, however, they were local concerns, employing local staff to serve local people - and thereby playing their part in the local economy.

It was proudly claimed that anything the people of Norwich - and, indeed, Norfolk - wanted could be purchased in Magdalen Street or St. Benedict's. There are still many people of more mature years who can recall the seething mass of shoppers who jostled their way along, especially on Saturday afternoons, to make their purchases from their favourite stores. And, all the while, the trams clattered their way up and down the streets, adding a general air of organised chaos to the scene.

A few of those stores still survive, but most have now become just memories of a past age. Each must have its own story to be told, and one that springs to mind is that of Walter Little and Sons, Gentlemen's Outfitters.

Walter Little, it must be admitted, was not a local man by birth, having come from Dorking in the 1890s to take up employment with that other renowned outfitting establishment, Green's on the Haymarket. However, he was a readily adopted son, for he took a full part in the life of the City, built up his little clothing empire here and raised a fine Norwich family, some of whom, happily,

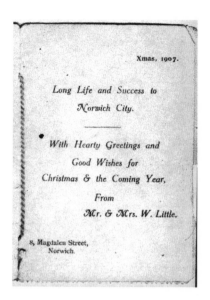

Walter Little's Christmas Card in 1907, just as the Canaries turned
professional and made their new home at 'The Nest'

are still here, as truly Norfolk as any of us.

He became an ardent supporter of Norwich City Football Club
and, as early as 1907, his Christmas Card to friends and special
customers bore, on the front, a yellow and green portrayal of a
canary standing on a football and, inside, his Christmas wish with
the words 'Long Life and Success to Norwich City,' It was the
very year that the Canaries, having turned professional, had
changed from their former blue and white shirts to yellow and
green and left their Newmarket Road ground for their new home
at 'The Nest.'

Walter Little was a tall, erect man, always impeccably dressed,
with hair brushed back and moustache neatly trimmed, smart
overcoat and, to complete the picture, a dark Homburg hat and
polished walking stick. One cannot help thinking that he must have
fitted well into George Green's scheme of things on the
Haymarket. All the while, however, Walter cherished the dream
that one day he might own his own store.

Then, in 1898, his dream became reality when he left Green's
and opened his own small business in Colegate. There he remained
for three or four years before transferring to Nos. 98-102

Walter Little & Sons' branch in St. Benedict's Street, Norwich.

St. Benedict's Street. The move was an instant success, and soon he was looking to extend his business. On June 27th 1907, he opened another store - at Nos. 8-10 Magdalen Street - and it was this that was to be, in present-day parlance, his flagship store and the hub of the little empire he was creating. A short distance away, on the other side of the street, he opened the smallest of his shops, next door to Loose's and always known as 'The Collar Box.'

Even this was not the end of his aspirations, for he opened up another outlet in St. Benedict's Street and, as the years went by, he extended his empire out into the county with branches in a cluster of busy little market towns. Thus, the menfolk of Watton, Wymondham and Diss could avail themselves of his services on their very doorsteps.

By this time there was much justification for the claim that 'LOTS ARE DRESSED BY LITTLE'S,' which later became the backbone of the firm's advertising.

That phrase is generally believed to have been the brainchild of Walter's son, Frank, and many will remember the hoarding, carrying that message, which stood for years above the River End Stand at Norwich City Football Club's ground at Carrow Road. A professional photographer was commissioned to photograph the

The firm's advertising slogan, standing above the crowd at Carrow Road's River End Stand.

The staff outing to Horning, July 1934. Walter is flanked by his three sons, with Charles on the left of the picture and Frank (with child on his lap) and Jack on the right

scene on an actual match day and, looking at the number of men wearing flat caps, one cannot help wondering how many of those caps were actually purchased from Little's.

I have described Walter Little and Sons as 'a family business,' and it certainly was that - in more ways than one. To begin with, Walter had three sons - Frank, Charles and Jack - and they all played their part, together with other family members, not least the renowned 'Aunt Fan.' The extent of the business, however, demanded that many other people be employed and they all soon became members of a kind of extended family working together for the good of the firm. On one day every year Walter expressed his gratitude to his mixed family by taking them on a staff outing.

In July, 1934, the venue was at Horning where, after a meal at the Swan Hotel, they gathered together outside for a group photograph to mark the occasion. Sadly, that may well have been the last photograph ever taken of Walter Little for, just two months later, on September 17th, he died, at the age of 62, leaving his empire in the hands of his sons.

The business he had created continued to prosper for a further twenty years, but then, almost imperceptibly, clouds were beginning to gather as people's tastes started to change. Then came the era of the sixties and, with it, the arrival of branches of the national chain stores. The little family shops began to lose their customers. The new generation of shoppers were more interested in designer labels and modern trends in fashion.

One by one, the little family shops of Magdalen Street and St. Benedict's, including Walter Little's, were forced to close down. By 1965 it was all over. Of the three brothers, Charles had already left to become a commercial traveller, Frank welcomed the chance of more time to engage in the social life of the City, which was his great joy, and Jack became landlord of the Hoste Arms at Burnham Market for several years until he retired.

One part of Walter Little's empire which continued to operate was the branch in Wymondham, taken over as an independent concern by Walter's grandson, John, who carried it on until his untimely death on September 5th 1991.

Now, all that is left is the memory of a man who came from Surrey with a vision, turned that vision into reality and, in so doing, became, if not exactly a legend, at least a significant figure in the history of the City of Norwich.

CHAPTER 10

Stand-Ins To The Stars

To those of us with a love for Norfolk, be it inborn or acquired, it is a pleasurable thought that increasing numbers of film makers are looking in our direction for locations to enhance their work. Then, when each completed creation gets its public showing, we eagerly identify the various settings and glow with a degree of smugness over the beauty which we had always known was there.

At the same time, however, it is pleasing to remember a film which, though made in the Cotswolds, owed its very completion to the timely presence of a couple of erstwhile residents of Norfolk.

It was in 1944, with the Second World War still raging, that somebody at one of the government Ministries hit upon the idea of a propaganda film which would demonstrate to the World that, despite bombing, rationing and all the other deprivations of the conflict, the people of Britain were ever ready to offer succour to refugees from other troubled countries. In short, it was to be a film about refugees and the manner in which they were received in our country.

We had regularly been treated to propaganda films urging us to do such things as digging for victory and handing in everything from pots and pans to iron railings to be transformed into weapons of war. These, however, were short and cheaply made affairs; the new project was to be very different. With overseas distribution in mind, national prestige was at stake – at least, as far as the financial situation would permit.

That, then, was the Ministry's great plan. There then remained the question of finding somebody to put it into action, and their choice was little short of a stroke of genius. The chosen man was Bernard Miles, one of the best-loved actor-directors of that era and a man destined, later in life, to be elevated to the Peerage. His cheery manner and rich Hertfordshire accent endeared him to cinemagoers and, furthermore, he was a man who, when confronted with a problem, always seemed to come up with a sudden rush of inspiration to overcome it.

He set about devising a plot for the film, and it was then that the first problem arose – which country should his refugees come from? Which nationality would best represent all the troubled countries of the world? Then came the inspiration. Why need the refugees be human beings? Why not members of the animal kingdom? Indeed, why not birds?

His fertile imagination soon provided the basic plot – a pair of rare birds, previously unknown here, come to Britain and make their nest in the countryside near the fictional Cotswold village of Lipsbury Lea. His choice of the Cotswolds stemmed partly from his long affection for the area and also from the fact that his brother was a teacher of maths at a school in nearby Chipping Norton and could hopefully help in the selection of possible locations. Bernard Miles' knowledge of ornithology was limited, but there happened to be one species of bird which had a name that appealed to him. That bird would be his choice – and the name of the film would be *Tawny Pipit*.

The overall plot for the film was flimsy in the extreme. As the news of the birds' arrival in Lipsbury Lea spreads through the birdwatching fraternity, the village community bands together to protect them, ably led by a retired army colonel – one of the kind always described as 'peppery' (the part destined to be taken by Bernard Miles himself). Young local lads suspend their normal bird's-nesting activities in order to join the protection parties, and the local vicar offers praise to the heavens with a new hymn to be sung in his church:

It's a very great honour, we're all agreed,
That they came to Lipsbury Lea to breed.

Then, on to the scene comes a Methodist minister with a professed dedication to the world of birds and a burning desire to be allowed to see the rare visitors. Soon, however, he is exposed as an impostor – an egg-collector with the sole intent of raiding the nest under cover of his cloth.

But, once that danger is disposed of, a new and much greater threat to the pipits rears its head. At the time when *Tawny Pipit* was being filmed, armed forces all over southern Britain were preparing for the landings in Normandy and the opening of the Second Front, and tanks were active in almost any sufficiently large area of unpopulated land. Hence, in the film, the plot reflected real life.

A squadron of tanks suddenly arrives and starts manoeuvring in the very area chosen by the pipits to raise their young. All seems lost, for surely this activity must inevitably destroy the birds and their nest before the eggs can hatch. But the Colonel is not a man to accept defeat lightly and, even more peppery than usual, he gets in touch with the War Office and appeals for the tanks to be diverted elsewhere. The response, not surprisingly, is initially one of incredulity that such a request should be made for the trivial matter of allowing a pair of birds to bring their young into the world. Gradually, however, the men from the Ministry mellow and, acknowledging the need to bolster civilian morale, the tanks are moved to another area.

Throughout the film, the Colonel is enthusiastically supported by a young couple who just happen to be in the village at the time. They are an RAF pilot, recovering from injuries sustained in aerial combat, and the nurse who has come to the village to tend him through his convalescence. Bernard Miles knew that the film would not succeed without a love interest, and this was admirably supplied by Rosamund John and Niall MacGuinness, and, while the incubation of the pipits' eggs proceeds, so romance between the human couple develops.

Even then, however, Bernard Miles felt that the film needed another element for, though he knew it to be a low-budget production, it was a matter of prestige and, furthermore, it was required to run for something approaching an hour and a half. Hence, a strange character suddenly appears in the village in the form of a Russian girl sniper (played by Lucie Mannheim) who proceeds to address the villagers of Lipsbury Lea from a farm cart in the shelter of a large tree. Her presence clearly has no connection with the main plot of the film, but her stirring account of Russian resistance to attack by German armies, together with glowing references to the bond of friendship which existed between her country and Britain, had great propaganda value. After all, we were friends at that time. We were fighting on the same side!

So the plot progressed and steadily worked its way towards a happy ending – cinemagoers always loved happy endings.

The tawny pipits hatch their eggs and introduce their fledglings to the new world which awaits them; the village community is filled with a surge of almost parental pride; and the young nurse marries her brave RAF patient in the now bomb-damaged village church. In the final scene, as they stand before the altar, the bride inclines her head and looks upward through the remaining rafters of the roof to see a flight of RAF planes making their way across the sky.

That, then, was the script that Bernard Miles prepared, but, as he wrote it, he was greatly troubled by the biggest of all his problems – where could he find the two principal characters of the story? It was essential that a pair of tawny pipits, complete with nest, should appear in the film, but his talents as an ornithologist did not match his skills as an actor and director. Hence, he sought advice from the foremost British naturalist, Julian Huxley.

The response was not encouraging, for the tawny pipit, he was told, was a lover of sandy wasteland and not likely to be attracted to the Cotswolds. A pair had been recorded as having nested in Sussex in 1905, but their favourite nesting place was on the dunes of France and Holland. All was not lost, however, for Huxley was able to suggest a bird that might double as the real thing. It was, in fact, a close relative, the meadow pipit. The colouring was slightly different but, as the film was being shot in an almost sepia-like tone, nobody would be any the wiser. Where, then, could he find meadow pipits?

"Norfolk," was the reply. Meadow pipits are great lovers of habitats around large sheets of water, and Huxley knew that several pairs were, at that moment, nesting in the rushy margins of Hickling Broad. Bernard Miles sprang into action and a film crew, armed with hand-held cameras to enable them to approach their subjects, headed for Hickling. Once there, they sought accommodation at the Pleasure Boat Inn, where they received a warm welcome and were enticed into sampling the local brew. Unaware of its potency, however, they seem to have imbibed rather too freely, with the result that, when the next day dawned, they did not possess quite the degree of steadiness required for hand-filming. Nevertheless, with the help of Britain's foremost bird photographer, Eric Hosking, they got their film, which was sent speedily on its way to Lower Slaughter.

The film was duly completed and offered to the cinema-going public in the summer of 1944, just as Allied forces were landing in Europe to open up the Second Front. I recall seeing it in a Naval Dockyard cinema in the south of England a year or so later and feeling in accord with the London critic, Richard Mallett, who considered it "an entertaining, quiet, rambling, very English

How J.H. Dowd, the *Punch* illustrator, saw some of the principal characters in *Tawny Pipit* when it was first shown in London in July 1944.

picture." At that time I was unaware of the vital part played by the two Norfolk residents who became stand-ins for the stars – I have a feeling my enjoyment would have been even greater with that knowledge.

One wondered what sort of effect *Tawny Pipit* would have on American audiences, and it was not until several years later that, as the result of an unexpected stroke of good fortune, we were to find out. A copy of the film had found its way to a movie-theatre on Forty-Second Street in New York where, having been dismissed by the proprietor as "a British film about a Goddam bird," it had lain in a cupboard unscreened. Then, one day in 1947, the same man found himself without a new film which he had been expecting to screen and, being without a substitute, he resigned himself to putting *Tawny Pipit* before his audience. The response was quite amazing. The people of New York took it to their hearts and it ran at the same cinema for several months.

I know of just one discordant voice – that of the female critic of the *New York Sun,* who complained that "The English are now sending over their old war propaganda films" and went on to deplore the sequence in which "A Russian woman sniper makes a speech, children sing the Internationale in English, and the village squire gives the Communist salute."

The *New York Times,* however, received it with great warmth. "Seldom," wrote its critic, "does such a piece of unsophisticated charm and humour reach the screen, but this one is presented in such an utterly beguiling fashion that it would be a grave error not to see it... It is an allegory of strangers who came to England during the war, seeking refuge, and despite certain prejudices and accidental obstacles were finally accepted by a basically warm-hearted and sympathetic people."

The *New Yorker* summed it up thus: "The picture tells how a placid English village is jarred from somnolence during the war by the arrival of a pair of rare pipits, which have to be protected while nesting from such dangers as manoeuvring tanks and thieving ornithologists. The subject is, Lord knows, bursting with whimsy, but somehow Bernard Miles and Charles Saunders, the co-directors, have kept the piece gently humorous and almost entirely avoided stickiness."

And all the while, it seems, nobody found out that the Cotswold pipits were, in reality, their waterside cousins from Norfolk.

3

A Posy of People

CHAPTER 11

Country Town Characters

Henry Bidewell - Builder

Henry Bidewell was, in his own estimation at least, one of the last 'real' builders in Norfolk. Starting his working days as a bricklayer in Wymondham, he went through life building up a business based on quality and trust until, in 1933, Kelly's Directory referred to him as 'builder and contractor; stone, marble and monumental mason & brick manufacturer & undertaker.'

Henry - always known to the locals, with typical Norfolk economy of pronunciation, as old Henry 'Byedle' - was short and stocky, with a tendency to portliness. His manner of dress was invariably that which proclaimed his position in society - a Norfolk jacket, breeches, leather buskins and brown boots. And, of course, he always wore a bowler hat, for that was the symbol of his place in the scheme of things. During his days as a bricklayer, it was a flat cap - only right and proper - but, when he became 'the guvnor,' the only appropriate headgear was the bowler. Then, completing his ensemble, there was his black stick with the silver knob - he and his stick were seemingly inseparable.

Henry had his yard in Middleton Street, and there, in the office, sat Frances Peacock, his clerk and book-keeper, whilst out in the yard was his stonemason, none other than Frances' father James.

James Peacock was a master of his craft. Quite apart from his inherent ability, he possessed a seemingly endless supply of patience. It was an age when time in the workplace had little of the significance that it has in today's hurly-burly world of business, and his master would never have urged him to work more quickly. Quality was the watchword. It is not surprising, therefore, that when, in 1919, the decision was made to erect a memorial to the men of Wymondham who had lost their lives in the Great War, James was the man chosen to engrave their names.

It was a mammoth task, for there were no less than 143 names to be inscribed, and one can only marvel at the length of time it must have taken to complete. The names were to be inscribed on four large tablets of stone, which would then be erected in box-like fashion, with each individually facing a different point of the compass.

The days went by, and James, having completed two tablets, was nearing the end of the third when he suddenly lost the power to carry on. He had completed 99 names but, as he faced the next one, his hands began to shake and his confidence in his ability evaporated. He dared not continue lest he should spoil all the fine work he had already done.

One might have thought that it was the sheer size of his task that had overcome him, but it was not so. It was, in fact, the next name, the hundredth on the list, which threatened to defeat him. He had been overcome by a strange mixture of pride and grief, for it was none other than that of his own son, Sidney, killed during the Battle of the Somme and now lying in the British War Cemetery at Hermies Hill in France.

He eventually completed his task, but he never forgot the ordeal of carving his own son's name. The memory was handed down through the family and was told to me by my friend, Ted Fowler, the old man's grandson. Today, the memorial, still lovingly cared for, continues to look out over Town Green, commemorating not only the bravery of the men whose names it bears, but also the skill and dedication of the craftsman who put them there.

The yard and the stonemason's workshop, however, were not the limit of Henry Bidewell's empire, for he had his own gravel pits in Chapel Lane and he made his own bricks in the old brickyard off Pople Street. Then, when it came to a question of timber, he would seek out the best from various local estates, and he took great pride in the oak that he used for doors, windows and staircases. In Henry's book there was no substitute for quality.

Though dedicated to his trade, there were moments when his gentle sense of humour would shine through the everyday round of business matters. There was, for instance, the fun he had with a pet tortoise which lived on the premises. Ted Fowler recalls the old boy's habit of slipping it under his hat on the desk when people came to see him, and then delighting in the expressions of incredulity on their faces as the hat began to move slowly across the desk as though driven by some unseen force.

I suppose Henry's major handicap was that he failed to move with the times. He never learnt to drive a motor vehicle, but he

Private Sidney James Peacock, 235337, 1st/4th Battalion Seaforth Highlanders, killed in action on the Somme, December 4th 1917, son of James and Hannah Peacock of Vicar Street, Wymondham

Wymondham War Memorial, 1919. Not a single poppy in sight - the British
Legion did not come into being until 1921

was quite happy to walk to his building sites if they were within reasonable distance of his office. On occasions when they were too far from town, he would go in the lorry when the materials were delivered, sitting next to the driver with his stick between his legs and both hands resting on the silver knob.

He never took kindly to the telephone, but he had one installed for prospective customers to contact him on Wymondham 59. He, however, felt that meeting face-to-face was the most civilised way of doing business. Both parties could weigh each other up, and then there were just three stages to go through - discussion, agreement and a firm handshake. That was how he liked doing business, and a large proportion was carried out during his regular Saturday afternoon visits to Norwich. And they were not completed without a degree of conviviality!

He would walk down to Wymondham station and, before boarding the train, would make a special point of giving the porter half-a-crown to make sure he got off the last train from the city that night and to help him into a taxi for home. He knew from long experience that he would most likely be in no fit state to carry out those manoeuvres unaided!

He invariably had two main ports of call on those Saturday visits, both highly popular places with people of Henry's ilk. For liquid refreshment he made for Back's establishment on the Haymarket and, for a meal, the not-far-distant Curat House.

There he usually had a table by the window, and it seems certain that much business was carried out at that table, for all his friends and suppliers knew where to find him. Even more importantly, however, they knew he was a man to be trusted, a good payer who liked to settle up before he gave them orders for the next week.

In his earlier years, his business jogged along at a steady pace and his reputation gave him a sense of security. During the 1930s, however, threatening clouds appeared on the horizon in the form of Norwich building firms which, rapidly increasing in size, began to stretch their tentacles ever outward to places like Wymondham. Henry was appalled at the prospect. He objected to outside firms invading the town - local builders, he felt, were quite capable of building houses for local people. Unfortunately, however, there was only one way in which he could beat them, and that was a matter of price. Hence, when one of the Norwich firms quoted a price for a house, Henry would step in and build it for less. But it was to bring about his downfall.

His first wife had died and he had married his book-keeper, Frances Peacock, and moved into a house in Folly Road. It was not long, however, before he fell sick and, just before the Second World War he died. It was then that the awful truth was revealed for, when all his financial matters were settled up, it became apparent that he had lost everything in his efforts to keep the invaders at bay.

Henry Bidewell's firm died with him and the business was taken over by the Macro brothers from Old Buckenham.

Leslie Fiske - Barber

Les Fiske was a barber, plain and simple. I doubt whether the word 'hairdresser' had come into use when he started his business in 1908 and, even if it had, it was not the kind of fancy name he would have given himself. The menfolk of Wymondham and the surrounding villages came to him to be shaved and shorn, and that was the service they got.

He carried on his business in the front parlour of the family 'two-up, two-down' house in Damgate Street, with old Bob Barnard living next door and the *Rose and Crown* public house standing hard by. Like so many similar establishments of the period, that parlour was an entirely male preserve, untrodden by female feet - even those of his wife. He had an ornate brass urn with a gas ring underneath to heat the water for shaving, a copious supply of pages from the *News Chronicle* neatly cut to size for lather papers, and a couple of cut throat razors, well-stropped and ready for use.

Yet it would not be true to say that the men who congregated within those walls received merely the two services of shaving and haircutting, for there was a third which he offered entirely free of charge. This was entertainment, for Les Fiske was a wondrous story-teller, and it is largely for that talent that he is still remembered. He had a seemingly limitless fund of anecdotes, many involving local people and so full of detail that his listeners were never quite sure whether they were true stories or the product of his fertile imagination. But, be they fact or fiction, many of his customers, after having received attention in his chair, would sit down again by the wall in the hope of hearing more, and this did not always help to boost his business. Frequently, a new customer would partially open the door and, seeing what appeared to be a queue of waiting men, he would then close the door and depart with a hurried "I'll try again later," before Les could explain the situation.

Before he opened his shop in the front parlour in Damgate Street, Les Fiske had worked for another barber. When he started in business on his own account, however, he acquired a status which set him a bit above ordinary workers, and he soon began to yearn for the one symbol that would proclaim that status to his fellow-men. He dearly wanted a bowler hat.

Before long, his yearning was not to be denied, and he made his way along Market Street to the local branch of 'Walter Little, Gents' Outfitters,' where one of his customers, Peter Bullivant, was manager at the time. Then, having made his purchase, he returned to his shop, proudly wearing the bowler for all the world to see.

But it was then that another problem arose, for where would he hang it when not in use? He had no wish for it to be mixed up with all the family's coats and jackets in the house, and he cringed at the mere thought of it sharing the hatstand in the shop with his customers' caps and scarves. Quickly, the decision was made. It would have a nail to itself, in the wall of the shop adjoining Bob Barnard's house.

Then began the search for a suitable nail and, after sorting through the vast array of nuts, screws, washers and bolts which had been accumulated in a variety of tins over the years, a satisfactory one was found. It was, to be truthful, a far better nail than was needed, for it was at least seven or eight inches long, but this meant that he could knock it well into the wall and leave just an inch or two protruding. So, with a few hefty clouts, the nail was driven into place and Les, hanging his precious bowler in its place of honour stood back and viewed his handiwork with a great feeling of satisfaction. As he stood there, however, he was blissfully ignorant of the fact that the wall, being of mere lath and plaster construction, was only a few inches thick, which meant that the sharp end of the nail was protruding an inch or more into Bob Barnard's front parlour next door.

Old Bob failed to notice it at first, for his eyes had grown a bit dim with the passing of the years. When he did eventually spot it, he pulled up a chair and climbed up to investigate - and he was rather pleased with what he saw. Of course, he had no idea where the nail had come from, and he wondered why he had never noticed it before, but he was an ardent collector of old clocks and was always looking for new places to hang them. He wondered why the nail had been knocked in backwards, but he could soon get his pliers and bend the point upwards, and that would prevent the clock from falling off. He fetched his pliers, carried out the task, and then hung up the clock. Then, just as Les Fiske had done earlier, he felt decidedly pleased with himself.

The years went by and there the nail remained, steadfastly carrying out its dual purpose. All through the 1920s and into the early 1930s it carried Les Fiske's bowler hat on one end and Bob Barnard's clock on the other. It was then, however, that Les decided to move his business to a shop in Market Street.

It was not a very long move - barely a hundred yards - and they took everything on a handcart. Then, when the old place was finally cleared, Les Fiske's wife decided - as wives often do - to go back and have a last look round to make sure they were leaving it nice and tidy for the new occupants. Her mission completed, she returned to the new shop.

"Everything alright?" asked Les.

"Well, yes," said his wife, "except for one thing. That great old nail you put in the wall to hang your hat on. That look wholly unsightly. You'd better just get your claw hammer and go and draw that out 'afore they come."

Back went Les, claw hammer in hand, but, no matter how hard he tried, the nail refused to surrender. It had gone in easily enough, but he was not to know that old Bob had turned up the other end to stop his clock falling off. He pulled with all his strength; he banged at it with the hammer; then, taking him completely unawares, out came the nail, together with a huge chunk of plaster from the wall. Les, covered in a cloud of plaster and dust, fell backwards onto the floor whilst a simultaneous crashing sound from next door signalled the arrival of Bob's clock on the floor. A dog on the street started barking, glasses on the bar at the *Rose and Crown* danced up and down - and old Bob came shuffling round demanding retribution.

"You've been a long time," said his wife when he got back to the new shop.

"Yes," said Les. "Old Bob came round. He wanted to know the time."

Charlie Miles - Taxi Driver.

Charlie Miles was a simple man, in the nicest sense of the word. It is not that he had any degree of mental deficiency, but merely that he had left school at an early age with little scholastic ability and no high-flown ambitions for the future.

He knew his place in society and he lived his life within it.

Charlie found employment with two unmarried sisters, the Misses Mallows, who ran a Temperance Hotel in the middle of town. His duties were those of a general handyman, cleaning the 'brights,' filling and trimming the oil lamps and bringing in wood and coal for the fires. Needless to say, the two sisters were teetotal, and they steadfastly demanded similar abstinence, not only from their staff, but also from the hotel guests. Charlie and his workmates obeyed the rules, although whether they continued that abstinence at the end of the day's work is exceedingly doubtful.

If his life's work had been confined merely to the tasks of an odd-job man, there can be little doubt that, by now, all recollection of the man would have faded into oblivion. There was. however, another duty he carried out - that of a taxi driver - and it was this activity which has caused his memory to linger.

The taxi was, in fact, a model T Ford, owned by the Mallows sisters and used for various purposes. Firstly, Charlie would drive it to the railway station to collect prospective guests and transport them to the hotel and, at the end of their stay, take them back to the station to board the train for home. Then, when his employers wished to make a business trip, he was at the wheel. Finally, there was its use in the conventional style of a taxi. Passengers could book it, with driver, to go to their requested destination, and Charlie would collect them, bring them back and, after collecting the fare money, hand it over to the Misses Mallows.

My colleague, Ted Fowler, recalls an occasion, somewhere around 1929, when he took a ride in the Model T. His grandmother had hired the taxi for the afternoon to take him, with his mother and brother, for a ride out into the countryside. He was a mere five years old at the time and it was the first time he had ever been in a motor car. He particularly remembers the wooden spoked wheels and the spare wheel and battery box on the running boards.

The family all sat in the back, with Charlie in the front concentrating on the driving. Ted has forgotten where they went, but remembers travelling down a tree-lined lane, suddenly coming upon a ford and the thrill of driving through the water. Later they came to a house, where they stopped and had tea and cakes. "Charlie seemed to be very friendly with the lady of the house," says Ted. "No doubt it was one of his regular stops."

If Charlie Miles had a fault, it was his gullibility. He lived in a world of trust and, being aware of this, there were always local lads who took great delight in playing practical jokes on him. There was the occasion, one dark night, when two of them booked him to take them to Ashwellthorpe. He duly picked them up and set off down the hill under the railway bridge, after which there is a sharp right turn, together with a much steeper incline, which slowed down the Model T to a modest walking pace. It was at this point that the two passengers quietly hopped out of the vehicle, leaving Charlie to carry on without them. History does not tell us how far he went before he discovered his loss, nor how the poor man managed to explain to the Mallow sisters why he returned without his passengers and, more to the point, with no fare money to hand over.

Even worse, however, was the night when they attempted to bring down the wrath of his employers on him. There were times when Charlie had to wait at the station for some time between trains, and it became known amongst the young men of the town that, at such times, he could easily be tempted into the *Railway Hotel* for a 'quick one.' Indeed, he always carried, somewhere about his person, a packet of Parma Violets to mask any suggestion of alcoholic aroma that might subsequently linger on his breath. So the young men hatched their plot. They would invite him to join them for a drink and one of their number would slip quietly away to go and fetch Miss Mallows.

The scene was set and Charlie was enjoying his drink when the door flew open and in burst the informer.

"Look out, Charlie," he shouted. Miss Mallows is outside and she's heading this way."

Poor Charlie was immediately overcome by sheer, utter panic.

"Oh dear," he wailed, "whatever shall I do? She mustn't find me in here."

"Well, there's only one thing to do," said the informer. "You'll have to lie on the floor under that bench seat by the wall, and we'll all sit on it and she won't be able to see you through our legs."

Trustful as ever, Charlie did as he was told, pausing just long enough to pop a Parma Violet into his mouth.

Almost immediately, the door opened and in walked Miss Mallows.

"All right," she said "Where is he?"

At that, the four men rose to their feet in unison, revealing the pathetic, panic-stricken figure of Charlie on the floor.

"There he is, Ma'am," said the informer. "Just like I told you - on the floor, dead drunk."

Once again, any sequel to the story remains unrecorded, except that he stayed in his job - and he made a vow never to drink in the *Railway Hotel* again. And he never did - at least not until after he had retired from his employment at the Temperance Hotel.

'Latter-day' Cox, one of the old-time fishermen of Sheringham photographed by Olive Edis in her delightful series of 'Sheringham Salts.'

These two quaint-looking characters are Sally and Jimmy Auger, who lived in a hut on Edgefield Green, just outside Holt, in the early 1920s. They earned their living from the land, working for local farmers, and Sally was said to be the equal of any man. She certainly looks the part, with a man's cap tied on with a headscarf, a long apron made of sacking – and a somewhat lethal-looking reap-hook in her hand.

A certain air of mystery surrounds this picture of a couple who went round the streets of Norwich selling vegetables and flowers. It is known that the photograph was taken in Norwich, but nobody has yet been able to identify either the location or, in fact, the identity of the couple.

This picture of an early unidentified female 'postman' also poses a few questions. Dressed in her normal outdoor clothing, with just an armband to indicate her status, could she, perhaps, have been filling the gap left by a male colleague away on duty at the Western Front?

Shoeblack. A photograph thought to have been taken under the arched doorway to Pollock's stables in Orford Place, Norwich, early 1900s.

Two Cromer lifeboat legends. Henry 'Shrimp' Davies stands by the clifftop memorial to his uncle, the renowned Henry Blogg, whom he succeeded as coxswain in 1947. 'Shrimp' was a worthy successor, being awarded the B.E.M. in 1970 and, when he retired in 1976, becoming the subject of the television programme, 'This Is Your Life.'

CHAPTER 13

The Man Who Went Nowhere

Frank Skelton is an out-and-out Yorkshireman. In fact, his roots are firmly embedded in the north-eastern moorlands of his home county – the very moors which gave him birth. Having said that, I feel an explanation is needed as to why a Yorkshireman should appear in a book about Norfolk folk.

There are several reasons. Firstly, true natives of both counties share at least two characteristics. Each has in his nature a streak of stubbornness – call it cussedness, if you like – and both have a marked disinclination to leave the county that spawned them. In Frank's case, it was two younger relatives, coming south for reasons of employment, who, 'being cruel to be kind,' considered they should bring him with them so that they could look after him. He could have his own room, with all the keepsakes he had collected – a kind of granddad flat.

That is how he suddenly came to appear among us, little more than a hundred yards from my own home. Ours was a chance meeting, and I readily accepted his invitation to visit him. I soon realised that he was not a happy man.

"I've got nothing against Norfolk," he said, "I think it's a nice place – what little I've seen of it. But it isn't my home – I miss the moors."

The days went by, and Frank's yearning for the moors showed no sign of abating. He was a fish out of water, a man pining for the heritage of the county he had left behind.

Before long, his young relatives realised the mistake they had made, and soon he was on his way back to the county of his birth. I saw him the day before he left, his face wreathed in smiles. I was sorry to see him go, but I shared his happiness. And I was grateful for the story he had told me, for it is that story which explains the presence of a Yorkshire Tyke in a Norfolk book.

Frank Skelton was always content to watch the world go by. It could be said, in fact, that he helped some of it on its way, for, like his father, he devoted his working life to the railway service.

However, whereas his father had risen to the rank of senior inspector at the L.N.E.R's biggest marshalling yard (a position which, incidentally, carried with it the privilege of wearing a frock coat), Frank satisfied himself with becoming Station Master on a quiet branch line. He went there in 1940 and, even though the number of trains passing through on any one day rarely reached double figures, he stayed until it was closed in 1965. As he, himself, put it, he "was never a getter-on."

To the dismay of his father, he steadfastly turned down all chances of promotion, preferring to stay and tend the roses and sweet peas which helped to win the certificates for "Best Kept Station" which regularly came his way. He stayed put, ignoring the free travel passes to which he was entitled, and never once took a holiday. It is firmly believed that the only trip he ever made was when, armed with a packet of sandwiches, he made the 40-mile trip to Thirsk to revisit his childhood home. Even then, eating the sandwiches on the return trip, he was back in time to see the 4-30 through his station.

It was not until his father died that Frank Skelton realised just how little he really knew about the man who had sired him. Children of his era were kept in ignorance of so much, and asking questions about family matters was frowned upon. Then, as he had grown older, there never seemed to be the right time to talk with his father about anything other than railway matters. Now it was too late. All those questions that ran through his mind would remain forever unasked.

Thus it was that, on his retirement, he decided to write his own life story. Many old folk embark upon such a project – and for a variety of reasons. Frank's one aim was that his own two sons should not suffer, as he did, the anguish of all those unasked questions. So he set to work on what he called his *Journal*.

And it was his *Journal* that brought him briefly into my life when he was on the verge of his 95th birthday. It was a happy day for me, for here was a man of great contentment and, above all, a man with instant recall of people and incidents previously long forgotten. This was not a record of events and personalities that had shone out from newspapers, nor was it a life story in the true meaning of the word, for it was not a continuous narrative. Each time he sat down to record something from his past, some other chord would sound and whisk him off on a different journey leading him into another decade, travelling back and forth like some present-day time lord. All the while, his mood would be constantly changing from hilarity to utter tragedy and, as he wrote, he was surrounded by the simple belongings he had accumulated over the years.

There were photographs of trains – the steam sort, of course. Then there were his books – I would hesitate to call it a library, for they were a slightly odd assortment. On the shelf above him stood the beautifully bound Volumes 1 and 2 of *The Boy's Own Paper*. There were the *New Standard Encyclopedia* and the *New Treasury of Literature*, both of which had long outgrown the adjective that their titles shared. In between these elderly volumes there was a touch of modernity with James Herriott and the *A.A. Book of the English Countryside*. And, on a table beneath the bookshelf, there lay the symbol of his existence – the railwayman's peaked cap, emblazoned with the red and gold company crest and, tastefully embroidered in gold, the words Station Master.

As I sat down to read Frank Skelton's *Journal* I was immediately transported back more than a century in time, and it was not merely the subject matter that took me on that journey, but rather the style in which it was written. It was flowing, almost stately, prose – the sort of writing so much in favour with Victorian writers – and he was not afraid of using long sentences:

I was, I am told, born at York on November 9, 1905, at No. 5 Philadelphia Terrace off Albemarle Road, but since our family removed shortly afterwards to Market Weighton I have no recollection of my life in the city of York.

Note his use of the word 'removed'; and every now and then he treats us to little gems such as: "There lived at Sherburn in Elmet an irate bachelor." A slight touch of Trollope there, perhaps?

The two major influences in his life were, not surprisingly, his father and the railway company, but it was apparent that it was his paternal upbringing that had the greater effect on his early years. His father was a devout Methodist as well as a railwayman, preaching long sermons of doom and gloom and warning all who listened of the evil of alcohol.

Even now, Frank can recall the songs he sang in the Infant Class some ninety years ago. They were joyous and happy, with words like:

"The dream man's coming with his train of cars,
With moonbeam windows and with wheels of stars."

102

But he also remembers the Temperance meetings and the gloom as his father read extracts from Wesley's sermons and displayed morbid illustrations of a drunkard's liver from a book called *Alcohol and the Human Body*. The songs he recalls from those occasions expressed different sentiments:

"There'll be work for everybody
And there'll be a better day
When pubs are closed forever
And the drink is swept away."

Young Frank lived under the threat of eternal damnation, for, on the wall above the head of his bed, there hung a framed religious tract – 'The One Above Seest All,' tastefully entwined with red rambling roses. This, however, did not deter him from pulling the sheets over his head while he ate scrumped apples – and then disposing of the evidence by hurling the cores as far as he could through the open window.

But Frank's recall of the past was not without a touch of humour. He remembers the local cinema manager who maintained order among his young patrons at children's matinees by patrolling the aisles and cracking a whip. He recalls the occasion, during the Great War, when a trainload of German prisoners-of-war arrived at Thirsk station and a local woman, with a piercing cry of "Baby-killers," dashed across and set about them with her umbrella. And then there were the telegrams from his uncle.

Uncle Richard had taken upon himself the mantle of patriarch of the family and, whenever a new child was born, he would send a telegram advising the parents on suitable Christian names. Frank can remember his brother being born in 1912 and the telegram arriving: "Christen him David Lloyd George." They compromised by calling him Joseph Lloyd. Even before Frank's arrival there had been a telegram, for his elder sister had been born on February 28th, 1900, the day which had seen the Relief of Ladysmith during the Boer War. The content of the telegram was, perhaps, predictable: "Call her Ladysmith." They called her Ethel.

But there were tragedies that also found their way into his overflowing cascade of memories. He recalls seeing his first dead body back in 1912 when he was still only six years old. The family were living in one of a row of railway houses which were owned by the company and occupied by its employees. He vividly remembers being called indoors from his play just as the body of one such employee, a guard who lived a few doors further down the street, was carried by. It seems that a bundle of firewood intended for the waiting room fire had been found in the saddlebag of his bicycle, and he had been sacked on the spot. Then, unable to face the shame which he had brought upon himself, not to mention the loss of his company house, he had drowned himself in the nearby pond.

The railway was a hard taskmaster, but this did not deter Frank from his wish to make it his career, and 1921 saw him taking the entrance examination for the railway clerical service. It was a formidable task, for he was a mere sixteen years old and the nature of the exam seems to have been daunting in the extreme. There were three sections to be completed, the first two being maths and English, *with special attention to spelling and legibility.* Then came the part which surely would have proved too great a task for most present-day teenagers – or even people of more mature years, for that matter!

He was required to draw, completely unaided and from memory, a freehand map of the outline of England and Wales and then to mark the boundaries of the 52 counties and the position of their principal towns. Then he was to add all the rivers, ports and coalfields – and finally all the main-line railway routes.

He passed the exam and so began his life-long career with the London & North Eastern Railway Company. Then, for the next fifty or so years, his brain was busily absorbing the memories which were later to fill his *Journal.*

One part of that half-century which Frank recalls in the greatest detail, though with mixed emotions, was at the end of the 1920s when, as a 24-year-old parcels clerk, he found himself working on the night shift at Leeds railway station. It was a hectic phase in his career, for it was in the glory days when the rail service carried 95 per cent of all traffic throughout the country – and some 2,000 packages passed through Leeds parcels office every night.

Each one of those items had to be recorded in great detail, with both its arrival in the office and its eventual departure to the required destination meticulously listed in the Company's records. And all this was done laboriously by hand. No press-button technology in those days.

The parcels office was situated in a vast underground cavern, excavated beneath the platforms and sufficiently extensive to accommodate the vast array of items which passed through to all parts of Britain. Devoid of windows and relying purely on somewhat basic artificial lighting, the entire bunker must have had a distinctly Dickensian air about it, especially when one considers the nature of some of the 'packages' being booked in and out. Parcels came in all sizes and shapes, together with tea chests, boxes of fish and wooden crates with a diversity of contents. But Frank particularly remembered the coffins which passed through, sometimes with a small glass panel through which he could observe the face of the deceased occupant. The charge for sending a coffin by rail, he recalls, was one shilling a mile, but it was half-price for children.

At intermittent intervals there would be a package which, over the years, became so familiar that the office workers always knew its contents without any need for investigation. Its delivery label bore the inscription 'Haigh and Gill, Rope-makers,' together with the name of the official hangman, Albert Pierrepoint, and his home address in Lancashire. Frank and his colleagues always knew when another execution was imminent, for there was always a new rope for each occasion. After it had been put to use, it would be secretly cut into small pieces and, even more surreptitiously, sold off as souvenirs. Every profession, it seems, has its perks!

As I now try to conjure up in my brain an image of Leeds parcels office, there is one thing of which I am certain – Charles Dickens would have loved it!

But, of course, the so-called dead-stock presented few problems when compared with the huge population of live creatures which passed through the parcels office. There were the day-old calves, each contained in its own sack. The manager, obviously a man of humanity, made a point of releasing them and allowing them to wander tentatively around as they awaited collection by their new owners.

There was the poultry, often numbering as many as a thousand at a time. The hens were not much trouble but, even though not a single ray of daylight found its way into that underground bunker, the cockerels somehow contrived to produce a lusty dawn chorus, with one after another joining in an out-of-farmyard cacophony of sound.

Then there was the fur and feather contingent – the cats, rabbits and cage-birds travelling down from more northerly places in the hope of finding favour with the judges at championships in the south. It was the memory of an encounter with a champion cat from Newcastle which has remained forever etched in Frank's mind.

It was in the early hours of one morning, when there was a bit of a lull in proceedings, that he decided to inspect the contents of one of the crates. He knew that it was customary for the animal to be enclosed in a cage within the crate but, as he lifted the lid, he realised, to his horror, that on this occasion there was no cage. There was a sudden flash of fur as the Newcastle champion took off and, almost flying up the stairs, made its bid for freedom. Frank set off in hot pursuit but, reaching the outside world, he was just in time to see the animal disappearing in the distance at the far end of the long platform.

It was a moment of sheer panic for Frank. What on earth could he do to remedy the situation? It must be remembered that a stiff code of conduct was imposed upon railway company employees at that time. A man going on duty without wearing a collar and tie could be sent home; smoking while on duty within sight of members of the public could bring instant dismissal. The thought of what penalty Frank would face for his neglect of duty did not bear thinking about.

It was just as the depth of his despair had reached its lowest ebb that the inspiration struck – why not substitute another cat in the place of the runaway truant?

Carrying out the switch was much easier than one might have thought, for two cats were kept permanently in the parcels office for the sole purpose of controlling the rodent population. Their presence was officially recognised, and the Company's regulations even stipulated that one shilling a week was to be used in respect of each cat to provide all the milk they could drink. They roamed the office as they pleased, well-fed, well-exercised, sleek and healthy. Hence, Frank caught one of them, popped it in the crate and sent it on its way south to compete in the intended championship.

There then followed the long days and nights of tension as he waited for the axe to fall – but the expected complaint and probable claim for compensation never came. Not even a simple enquiry. Not a word from anybody!

"I wouldn't be surprised if it won," said Frank. "It was a good-looking cat."

He remembers it all as if it was yesterday. Indeed, he remembers everything as if it was yesterday.

A station master had living quarters within his station in those days, and Frank recalls one such man who seemingly lived all his life in his carpet slippers. The only concession he made to convention when a train came in was to put on his station master's peaked cap as he shuffled across the platform to see it on its way.

Then there was the passenger who regularly made the 20-mile journey from Leeds to the branch line station where Frank was in temporary charge. Nothing unusual in that, except that the man was always dressed in full hunting pink and was the only man who had the audacity to take over the station master's chair while he waited for his hunter to be unloaded from a horse box in a siding. Then, off the two of them would go to join the local Hunt for a day's sport. And Frank can even remember the fares – eleven shillings for the horse, and five shillings first class return for the rider.

Eventually, in 1940, Frank got his first permanent appointment, at a small station in the North Riding, midway between Scarborough and Robin Hood's Bay, overlooking the cold North Sea. It was Staintondale, a small, scattered village of barely 350 souls, and he took an immediate fancy to the place.

There was very little at Staintondale to disrupt the even tenor of everyday life; there were rabbits aplenty on Fylingdales Moor; and the North Sea brought ashore a variety of offerings, from the occasional box of oranges to the sealed tin of pyramid-shaped sweets adorned with Chinese writing which arrived one day. In the peace and quiet of the afternoons the station staff would wander off to shoot pheasants, and Frank would settle down to tend his roses and all the rest of nature's offerings which marked his station out as, if not the biggest, at least the best-kept.

So the years went by and the railway continued inexorably on its way, but eventually Frank realised that all was not well. The trains travelling along that coastal line were steadily becoming perceptibly fewer in number. Then, at Christmas in 1964, when he once again won the award for the Best Kept Station, they told him to take the £5 prize money from his ticket takings – but it was the end of February before the fare money was sufficient to cover it!

Then the inevitable happened. It was 1965 and Dr Beeching was wielding his axe. The line was closed and the rails were taken up. But what of Frank Skelton? Staintondale had not been just his home but his entire world for a quarter of a century. He had never gone anywhere, and he had no wish to start now. So he stayed put. At first he became the railway company's tenant, but later he

Staintondale station, with Frank's flower beds replacing the former railtrack.

was able to buy the station. And that was the point at which, in between tending his roses and keeping his little world tidy, he sat down and began writing his *Journal*. Once again, within his phenomenal memory, the Newcastle Cat made its dart for freedom, the Infants' classroom echoed with 'The dream man's coming' and Frank was drawing his free-hand map of England and Wales.

It was a simple twist of fate which brought this proud Yorkshireman briefly into my life, too briefly to really get to know him, yet long enough for his writings to tell me everything I could wish to know about him. It was never his wish that his *Journal* should be published, and, fascinating though it is, I must confess to a hope that his wish is respected. You see, I have an awful fear that some over-zealous editor might decide to put his narrative 'in order' and thereby deprive it of its splendid innocence.

Frank Skelton has now left his station and, as he himself would put it, removed to one of the cottages in the village. He still hears the sound of the North Sea, and he is within yards of the station where he tended the roses. Still the world passes by, leaving him with his memories – and his contentment. After all, he never was a getter-on!

CHAPTER 14

The Stalham Scorcher

There cannot be many towns and villages throughout the length and breadth of Norfolk which have not, at some time, numbered amongst their parishioners a local historian of some kind. In many cases their recordings may have been confined to such things as a church, a local business or a family of some repute. Others, however, have produced work on a grander scale. East Dereham had its long-serving Vicar, Benjamin Armstrong, Edgefield its own long-term cleric, Canon Marcon, while Diss had former headmaster Eric Pursehouse - all men of letters. In the case of Stalham, however, it was the local miller, W. H. Cooke, to whom we are indebted for so much knowledge of past happenings in that area.

William Cooke, it is true, was not a man of letters in the normally accepted sense, but he was an educated man with a marked talent for writing, and, what is more, he had three greatly differing outlets through which he channelled the output of his pen.

Firstly, there was his diary of happenings in the area which he kept, day by day, for 76 years from 1839 until he left the district in 1915. In it he reported events large and small, from the relief of Ladysmith in 1900 to the death in 1906 of Sally Pratt, who "possessed the 'Evil Eye' and was greatly feared as a witch," and from the death in 1881 of John Leatherdale, the last remaining stage coach driver in the county, to the introduction of a second postal delivery in 1884. Page after page of local information is there, soberly presented and ready to be seized upon by aspiring historians.

The second outlet for his writings was the *Eastern Daily Press,* for which he was the Stalham correspondent. In this medium, of course, he was dealing strictly with facts although there were occasions when certain people involved in his reports were not exactly enamoured with the way in which those facts were presented.

The third vehicle for William Cooke's writings was a kind of parish magazine which appeared every Thursday, price twopence. He was not only the founder and proprietor of this publication, but also its editor, printer and circulator. Furthermore, the fact that he was also its only writer gave him plenty of scope to broadcast his views on any topic, of which he had many! Its pages were packed with satirical pieces and lampoons of local people and committees. There was nothing really libellous in what he wrote and much of it was thinly veiled, though not sufficiently to conceal the identity of the person he was writing about. He had no time for pomposity or self-opinionated people and delighted in cutting them down to size.

The name of the publication was *The Stalham Review - a Record of Town Topics* but, because of the nature of its content, it rapidly became known as the *Stalham Scorcher*.

Most of the people who found themselves lampooned in *The Scorcher* took it all in good part, but there were a few who did not, notably R. J. Perfitt, the Stonemason, and his eldest son, a veteran of the Boer War. When news had come of the capture of Pretoria in the Boer campaign, the people of Stalham had celebrated with a pageant in which the elder Perfitt played a major part as the Mayor of the captured Boer capital handing over the keys of the city to his British conquerors. This was an occasion for W. H. Cooke to seize upon and, henceforth, Mr Perfitt was always referred to in *The Scorcher* as 'The Mayor.'

Then, in 1902, the residents of Stalham decided to mark the Coronation of Edward VII by purchasing a new fire engine. Although new to Stalham, it was, in fact, second-hand, having previously seen service with the Woolwich Arsenal Fire Brigade, but, with 'Coronation 1902' and 'Stalham' emblazed on its sides, it was a proud acquisition for the local people and quite a bargain at £75. The idea was to have a ceremonial handing-over of the engine to the people, followed by a demonstration of its capabilities.

Sadly, on the very eve of his Coronation, the King was stricken down with appendicitis, and the Coronation was, of necessity, postponed indefinitely. In accordance with his wishes, however, and in common with the rest of the country, Stalham went ahead with its planned celebrations, though the sense of occasion was not what it would have been.

Unfortunately, in spite of the proximity of the river, Stalham had no central supply of water, and the fire brigade always had

110

to rely on a human bucket chain to the site of a fire until local farmers could be called in to bring water carts to service the pumps. The Midland and Great Northern Railway had been given permission to lay pipes from the river to their water tank at the station, and the Parish Council had proposed to extend the facility to a hydrant in the street. This, however, was never installed, for it was not considered fair to levy a rate on the whole parish for something that benefitted just the shopkeepers!

Hence, the new engine was taken out to the river near Hunsett Mill for the parishioners to marvel at the sight of the water being projected at 130 gallons per minute high above the sails of the mill, which stood at no less that seventy feet from the ground. But there were those among the assembled throng, not least William Cooke, who harboured doubts about the value of such a machine when faced with a genuine fire but without a ready supply of water.

His subsequent lukewarm record of the occasion was cause for much gossip in the parish. Furthermore, his description of the Fire Engine Presentation and its by no means flattering picture of "Our Mayor, commanding the chairman of the Parish Council to approach and receive the gift of the Coronation Engine," did not fall lightly upon the ears of the Perfitts.

Retribution was not long delayed. On the evening of August 6th, William Cooke answered a knock on his front door to find a workman with a message to say that his presence was required on a nearby road. Suspecting nothing, the sixty-year-old Cooke made his way to the appointed place where, waiting for him, he found the younger Perfitt. The young man's intentions were plain to see, for he was armed with a riding whip, with which he proceeded to attack Cooke, striking him with a torrent of blows 'on his upper legs and lower back.' Then, adding insult to injury, he forced his victim to sign an apology to be sent for publication in the *Eastern Daily Press*. His mission accomplished and his father's reputation - as he thought - restored, he strode off, leaving his victim to make his way painfully home. There Cooke found it necessary to take to his bed - lying face downwards - for the best part of a week, but his spirit was by no means subdued.

He immediately made it known that he intended to take legal action for damages against his assailant, and the entire parish was agog with excitement at the prospect of the coming litigation. In the end, however, he accepted the good council of friends and agreed to an out-of-court settlement of 'a sizeable sum' from the defendant.

Before many months had elapsed, the people of Stalham were able to observe their new fire engine in action in deadly earnest, for it was in the early hours of January 6th 1903 that the call came from Bristow's Mill. The owner, John Bristow, had woken up at 4 o'clock to the smell of smoke and, fearing the worst, had got his wife and children - of whom there were many - to a place of safety. Then off he ran along the road to the village, loudly crying out for the fire brigade - it was the only means of contact in those days!

But, once again, there was just one thing lacking - water! Fire Captain Howlett dispatched his 'knocker-up' to the nearest farm to summon water carts, while everybody set about moving the Bristows' furniture to a nearby field.

It was half an hour before the water carts arrived on the scene, and, by that time, the mill was lost. Having stood sentinel over the landscape for over a century, it had been wiped away almost as though it had never existed.

There was no lampooning from W. H. Cooke this time. His piece for the *Eastern Daily Press* bestowed great credit on Captain Howlett and his men.

But still there was no water, and the situation remained the same when Stalham suffered the most destructive fire in its history on November 6th 1906. Again there was the wait for water carts, with the men trying to combat the flames with buckets of water from a near-empty well. This time, however, there was added assistance from another source, for Dr Rudd had driven in his motor car to North Walsham to summon the men from that Brigade, and they responded by covering the eight miles in eighteen minutes. It was a case of too little too late, however, and by the time the fire was brought under control it had completely destroyed Arthur Hensman's grocery and drapery business - the largest in the High Street - together with the adjoining branch of Barclay's Bank. And it had all been brought about, in the opinion of Mr Hensman, by rats in the attic where he had stored large quantities of matches!

However, that was not the end of the story, for William Cooke tells us that the business-like Arthur Hensman hired the Town Hall and continued his business from there, while the equally business-like Fire Brigade, in the person of Captain Howlett, presented the Parish Council with a bill amounting to £174, which included the sum of £18. 16s. 9d. for refreshments. It was that latter item which became the main sticking point, for it was at a time when beer was just a penny per pint, and the regulations stated that each man should be limited to two pints per day.

When the matter came before North Walsham County Court there were many references to 'a beer orgy' and 'a drunken beano,' and the insurance assessor from London declared: "In all of my twenty years of experience, never have I seen such an account for settlement by an Insurance Company. During my stay in the village, beer was coming across the street from an Inn in a constant flow."

All the while, of course, W. H. Cooke was having the time of his life. He produced an extremely lengthy poetic work describing the actual fire fighting, liberally sprinkled with passages like:

As the fire raged on, the men gave cheer,
Sustained by the thought of unlimited beer.
The morning advanced, but none did shirk
Their part in the arduous, dangerous work.
Then the Captain, the Super, and Engineer
Went in for something stronger than beer.
They crossed the street, the three in a bunch,
And paid their respects to a glorious lunch.
Of this they partook with well-earned ease,
While the men filled their voids with bread and with cheese.

His report of the court case for the *Eastern Daily Press* was, of course, more respectfully presented. But in the pages of *The Stalham Scorcher* things were very different. What a heaven-sent opportunity for Mr Cooke. His brain was on to it in a flash - a parody on The Charge of the Light Brigade. Here is the final verse:

When can their glory fade?
O, the wild charge they made,
All the world wondered.
Honour the score they made,
Pay up - let it ne'er be said
In settling for beer, meat and bread
That somebody had blundered.

And the outcome? The Parish Council eventually won the day and costs were awarded against the Captain, but it was stressed that at no time was the Fire Brigade's competence to fight fires challenged - **only their capacity to consume beer.**

The month of May in 1911 had already started its course when Stalham's parish councillors began to think they should consider arrangements for the celebration of the Coronation of King George V. After all, the event was to take place on June 26th, and there was much preparation to be done.

Accordingly, a public meeting was held at the Town Hall, where suggestions came thick and fast - a celebratory meal, Coronation mugs for the children, bags of coal for the old folk, and so on. As with most such meetings, many ideas were put forward, but with each suggested event there came three problems - finding a site for it, calling for volunteer organisers and, most of all, finding the cash to finance the events.

In the June 15th issue of *The Scorcher* William Cooke went into verse to report the business of the meeting:

In the fair month of May in this year of grace
Loyal Stalham, with the rest of the nation,
In its wisdom resolved that it certainly would
Take its part in the King's Coronation.
Our Parochial Council at once took the lead
And met in our stately Town Hall!
The Ratepayers rushed with all possible speed
In order to "kick off the ball."
But e'er very long it was speedily seen
That suggestions were too freely made.
It was all very well to try and feed all
But the Piper would have to be paid!
And in the midst of talk, talk, talk,
The news came with a crash -
When the Treasurers of all the Clubs
Said "We haven't got the cash!!!"
At the close of the meeting they wisely resolved
To act as they do in the City -
Take account of suggestions and then hand them on
To be dealt with by a Committee.

It seems that the Committee managed to carry out its appointed task for, in the next week's issue of *The Scorcher,* we find:

June 22nd 1911 - Report of Proceedings.
Held in the grounds of the Royal Maid's Head Hotel, Stalham.

I suspect that the prefix 'Royal' was a tongue-in-cheek bestowal by Mr Cooke for, though the 'grounds' did retain a modicum of

The *Stalham Review* of June 15th 1911, carrying news of the last-minute arrangements for celebrating the Coronation of King George V.

grass and other greenery, they were also partially occupied by a variety of domestic and farmyard animals housed in structures concocted from odd pieces of wood and metal. Nevertheless, that was where the Coronation Celebrations took place and, thrusting his tongue even further into his cheek, this is how William Cooke described the event:

The members of the Coronation Committee are to be congratulated that one of their number placed at their disposal his charming grounds, now in the full splendour of their Summer beauty. The worthy, popular and patriotic proprietor has excelled himself in the artistic beauty of the decorations. His treatment of the range of pigsties is beyond praise. We are of the opinion that nothing in the Metropolis can excel them, the artistic draping of the corrugated iron was wondrous fine, the very animals behind rise above it in order to drink in the beauty of the scene. The patient ASS is also seen braying his cordial ASS-ent! The poet says "A thing of beauty is a joy for ever." As long as Reason remains seated on its throne, those decorated pigsties will remain an unfading memory. The romantic slaughterhouse of Messrs Merry rising above the umbragious foliage formed a pleasing southern boundary to the GROUND.

The fashionable and well-dressed crowd, immediately after

115

The Special Coronation Celebration Number of *The Scorcher*

Matins at the Parish Church, assembled and lent animation to the scene. The ladies' toilettes were simply ravishing - but as the magnitude of some of the ladies' hats evidently obstructed the view, sinister remarks were heard from some of the 'lower orders.' After the conclusion of the Sports an Alfresco Concert took place. The vocal items were marvellously rendered considering the cargoes of cold plum pudding taken on board. The instrumental numbers for the same reason displayed a lack of timbre! The gentle grunting of the SOW formed a soothing accompaniment, but the braying of the ASS had too much of the staccato, but he did his best.

As the shades of evening crept o'er the scene, the well-fed crowd dispersed and, as they left the grounds, we noticed that one and all glanced with admiration at The Decorated Pigsties!!!

The satirical manner in which that piece was written gives, I believe, a pretty fair indication that William Cooke and the proprietor of the Maid's Head Hotel were not exactly on the friendliest of terms. Further evidence of this was to come when a Press report stated that "At the Vestry meeting, the landlord of the Maid's Head complained of the screeching of the Church Owl."

This bird had long been in residence around the Church tower and was often to be heard making its presence known as it engaged in its nocturnal activities.

Sure enough, the following week, the columns of *The Scorcher* carried a defence of the bird, in poetic form and with an added inference as to the creature's specific party political persuasion!

THE OWL'S LAMENT.

On Stalham's noble cloud-capp'd Tower
The Owl for ages past
Has thrived in placid dignity
Above the withering blast
Of human spite and petty rage
And still would wish to live
In such a way as doth become
A good Conservative.

But, sad to say, my dignity
Of late hath been disturbed
In such a way unbearable
To me, a high bred bird,

117

For on a pole just opposite
At which e'en dogs do howl,
They've had the insolence to place
A wretched ill-stuffed owl!

They say where ignorance is bliss
'Tis folly to be wise.
Had Radicals insulted me
'Twould not have caused surprise
But how is it that such as you
Who pose as loyal people,
Defenders of the State and Church,
Can thus insult the Steeple?
Which long has been the residence
Of a Bird renowned in story
For wisdom, dignity and pride -
The Birthright of a Tory.

Rash mortals pause, amend your ways
By fair means or by foul.
Relieve my outraged feelings and -
Remove that hideous OWL.

The authorship of that piece was credited to one 'Minerva,' but it surely needs little stretch of one's imagination to detect the identity of Minerva's *alter ego*.

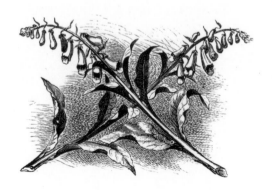

4

A Norfolk Miscellany

CHAPTER 15

The Solicitor's Tale

For something like fifty years I shared a warm and mutually satisfying friendship with the late William Bernard Gledhill, senior partner in the Wymondham firm of solicitors, Pomeroy and Son. His was a firm with a long pedigree and a wealth of history behind it, tracing its origins back in an unbroken line to the early years of the eighteenth century and now proudly boasting of being the oldest law firm in Norfolk.

Bernard Gledhill and I met quite frequently, sometimes socially and at other times when we attended a meeting of some committee or other onto which we had allowed ourselves to be coerced into serving. On those latter occasions, the part we savoured most was the coffee break, when we were free to exchange stories of the past. And what stories he had to tell! I have often thought that the inner recesses of Pomeroy and Son's offices must be a documentary delight, bringing alive the characters and lifestyles of over two centuries. All the world is there; at least, all the Norfolk world. The very names speak volumes, from the quaintly ancient like the late eighteenth century partner Jeremiah Burroughes and his pupil Jehosaphat Postle to landed gentry in the form of the Lombes of Great Melton Hall and the Routh Clarkes of Wattlefield.

Bernard spoke softly and deliberately, as if considering each word before he spoke it – probably part of his legal training. All the while, however, there was a glint in his eye as he anticipated my reception of his story, for he knew I was a ready listener. The stories he had to tell ranged from the oddly comical to the sensational. There was, for instance, the farm labourer who, having left school with no scholastic ability before he was fourteen, drifted into an arduous life on the land and later, while still a young man, sought advice on obtaining a divorce.

"On what grounds?" he was asked.

"Well, master Gledhill," he replied, "thass like this here. My marriage han't never been consumed."

At the other end of the scale, there was the part played by

Another committee meeting! The author is seated on the right with Bernard Gledhill standing behind him. The business of this particular meeting was the signing of the contracts for the building of Wymondham Central Hall.

members of the staff in the period before and after the notorious Rush murders, of which more later.

There can be little doubt that the success of the firm in its earlier years owed much to the manorial system which developed in feudal times and was recorded in 1086, with the Domesday Book indicating that the entire country had been divided into manors. Norfolk had its fair share, each one in the hands of its Lord of the Manor in his stately pile and with his demesne, or Home Farm. All matters concerning the running of the manor were negotiated by means of a manorial court, usually held in a solicitor's office or, perhaps, a local public house. Thus it is clear that stewardship of one such court could be a useful source of income to the solicitor who acquired it.

Wymondham and the surrounding area had a number of such manors, many with names that are still part of the local vocabulary, with some having been adopted as street names. The largest was Wymondham of the Queen, owned at one time by Queen Elizabeth I, who is recorded as having visited it on two occasions. Then there were Wymondham Hethersett, Choseley, Rusteyns and Stalworthy.

The location of the various manors was certainly well-known in the 1890s, for a story has been handed down concerning a young man named Ayers who came from Yarmouth to be a pupil with the firm. He took up accommodation in Market Street, at a point where several of the manor boundaries met, and legend has it that he would lie in bed at night and try to calculate in which manor various parts of his body were situated. He seems to have decided that when his left shoulder was in Wymondham Hethersett and his left hand in Wymondham of the Queen, his right hand would be in Rusteyn, his right foot in Choseley and his left foot in Stalworthy. A fanciful notion, perhaps, but probably better than counting sheep.

Another great source of income for the firm was the patronage of the Lombe family of Great Melton Hall. Sir John Lombe was a man of great standing in Norfolk in the latter part of the eighteenth century, with an interest in no less than thirty manors. He had inherited a large area of land in the Bawdeswell area and also acquired Belaugh Hall, near Wroxham – as the result of a gambling debt! He was known throughout Norfolk as one of the county dignitaries and, needless to say, he became a valued client, as did his family for a century or more.

It was while speaking of the Lombe connection that Bernard recalled an incident in which Mr Edward Lombe's gamekeeper, a certain John Skipper, played a prominent part. The year was 1827 and one day, as the evening wore on and dusk began to fall, Skipper was standing outside his cottage deep in conversation with John Archer, a shepherd also in the employ of Edward Lombe. Both men were honest, upright citizens, Skipper with an ever-present ambition to rid his master's land of the poaching fraternity and Archer with equal dedication to the estate. Poaching was a much more heinous offence in those days, with the sure certainty of a prison sentence for anybody found guilty, together with the destruction of his dog. It seems, furthermore, that a gamekeeper was within his rights to take a shot at any marauding dog running loose on his master's land.

As the two men talked, a light mist began to rise from the land, and it was then that they saw two figures approaching. They instantly recognised them as two unsavoury characters, John Pegg, described by a contemporary as "a chimney sweep, who rarely occupied himself in his calling but contrived to live by poaching", and John Standley, who already had a record of more than twenty convictions for similar offences. The gamekeeper and the shepherd watched with growing suspicion as the two passed by, a feeling certainly not lessened by the fact that the miscreants had with them two dogs, one of them being a lurcher – a breed much favoured by the poaching fraternity.

Then, seeing the men and their dogs turn into a narrow lane leading to a field and a patch of woodland, they decided to follow, stopping only long enough for John Skipper to fetch his gun. They turned into the lane and walked towards the field, but their quarry had vanished. They stopped and looked around, and then Skipper saw signs of movement in the undergrowth. "One of the dogs," he thought. "At least I can get him."

He took up his gun, aimed low into the undergrowth and fired. Almost immediately, a piercing shriek of pain echoed through the trees. Skipper ran to the spot to finish the animal off. But it was not the dog that he had hit. It was John Pegg, who had received a full round of shot in his lower back and hindquarters. He later ascribed the location of his wound to the fact that he was bending down at the time to remove a thorn from some unspecified part of his anatomy.

The case duly came before the court but, on this occasion, the usual roles were reversed, for the honest gamekeeper, John Skipper, was 'the prisoner in the dock,' facing a serious charge, and the unsavoury John Pegg was 'the prosecutor.' Unfortunately for Pegg, his reputation had preceded him, and 'the prisoner' was found not guilty.

John Pegg left the court in disconsolate mood, his tail well and truly between his legs, and headed for the Cock, a public house which was still in existence in Wymondham until comparatively recent times. There, the assembled drinkers, having heard the details of the assault on his person, offered to buy him a drink if he would show them his torso. To Pegg, the offer was too tempting to refuse. It was then that he had an inspiration. Wymondham was, at that time, a town almost bursting at the seams with pubs and ale-houses. Why should he confine his custom to the Cock?

Tradition has it that it was three weeks before he had to start paying for his own drinks again.

From tales of poaching and firearms, Bernard's thoughts inevitably turned to what must surely be the most outstanding case with which the firm has been connected – the Rush murders in 1848.

James Rush was originally an auctioneer in Wymondham, and the law firm had dealings with him over a period of many years. Later, however, he decided to go into agriculture in a rather big way, and it was undoubtedly this decision that was to bring about his eventual downfall. Added to this, he was a self-confessed womaniser, proudly boasting of his success with the opposite sex, though this boast must surely have been dented when, in 1839, he was sued by a woman for breach of promise. She claimed he had made her pregnant, as a result of which she had found it necessary to go into the workhouse. Her claim was upheld and he was ordered to pay financial recompense to the woman he had wronged.

In order to make his entry into the world of agriculture, Rush approached the incumbent of Stanfield Hall, a reverend gentleman named Preston, who owned various holdings in the area. Thus he acquired the tenancy of Potash Farm at nearby Hethel, another farm at Westwick, near North Walsham, and a third parcel of land at Stanfield. It is worth noting, perhaps, that, in 1844, Rush's stepfather was found dead by gunshot in the house at Felmingham. Rush was known to have been shooting there that day, but it seems

Stanfield Hall, scene of the notorious Rush murders.

that suspicion did not fall on him, and the inquest produced a verdict of 'accidental death.'

The beginning of the end for James Rush was signalled with the arrival of a new owner at Stanfield Hall in the form of a barrister named Isaac Jermy. Jermy was a highly regarded figure in the business and financial world of Norfolk, being Recorder of Norwich and, furthermore, President of Norwich Union Insurance Society. At first, Rush was happy to serve his mortgagee as bailiff, but it was not long before Isaac Jermy declared that the tenancy agreements previously in force were invalid and set about issuing new – and more stringent – ones. Writs and foreclosure orders began to be issued, with both the law firm and the bailiffs having a field day. Before long, Rush found himself left with only Potash Farm, but then came the last straw. It was a writ for £5,000, the amount of the mortgage on Potash Farm, an almost impossible amount for a tenant farmer to find at that time, and certainly not within Rush's compass.

One evening, late in November, the Jermy family of father, mother and son were preparing for dinner in Stanfield Hall, where the law firm partners, John Mitchell and Edward Palmer Clarke, were due to join them to draw up plans for the removal of Rush from Potash Farm. Those two men, however, had been delayed on business in London and were to be unable to return until the following day – a matter of some significance as things turned out.

One can only wonder at the state of the domestic plumbing in the Hall for, just as they were about to start their meal, Isaac Jermy found it necessary to rise from the table and go through the porch into the garden to relieve himself. Almost immediately, the sound of a gunshot was heard, and Jermy lay dead. Then the door flew open, and in came a hooded figure carrying a blunderbuss. It was James Rush, and he proceeded to fire three more shots, killing Mrs Jermy and wounding her son and a serving maid. Then he turned and made his escape.

Members of the local police force were soon on the scene, among them being John Secker, an employee of Mitchell and Clarke, in his capacity as a special constable. The next morning, James Rush was arrested and Potash Farm searched by a party which, coincidentally, included another employee of the firm, Edward Pomeroy – a man who was destined to figure highly in the history of the firm in later years.

The trial duly took place, with Rush conducting his own defence. It was plain from the outset that his chance of being acquitted was very small, and any hope that he may have harboured in that respect was dashed when his current mistress took the stand to give evidence. The woman in question was the heavily pregnant Emily Sandford, and she deserted him in his hour of greatest need, giving evidence which was described as 'damning.'

The jury wasted little time in finding him guilty of murder, and arrangements were put in hand for his execution. It was still the age of public executions and our forefathers must have had a morbid streak in their make-up, for they turned out in vast crowds, together with itinerant traders selling such things as refreshments and souvenirs. The entire staff of Norwich Union were given time off on this occasion to witness the last moments of the man who had murdered the President of their Company.

Furthermore, interest in the event was not confined to Norfolk, for every newspaper in the land had carried reports of the murder and subsequent trial, and special trains brought sightseers in from far and near. It is recorded that, on police instructions, a trainload of passengers from London was stopped at Attleborough and prevented from carrying on to Norwich.

A pottery firm in Staffordshire cashed in on the event by producing a set of six figurines representing the principal figures in the case, together with relevant buildings. They were likenesses of Isaac Jermy, James Rush and Emily Sandford, together with Stanfield Hall, Potash Farm and Norwich Castle, which was still serving as the local prison. They are now eagerly sought-after mementoes, for a set of which, I am reliably informed, collectors would eagerly pay several thousands of pounds.

Ever since the events of that tragic night, there has been a certain doubt in some quarters as to whether, when Rush went to Stanfield Hall with his gun, Isaac Jermy really was his intended target. Admittedly, Jermy was the prime cause of his downfall, but there are many, of whom Bernard Gledhill was one, who have strongly believed that the people he was really after were the two partners of the law firm, John Mitchell and Edward Palmer Clarke. Their belief is supported by evidence at the inquest which followed.

Firstly, there was the fact that, as he burst into the Hall after disposing of Isaac Jermy, he is recorded as having shouted out,

Edward Boyce Pomeroy

"Where are those damned attorneys?" He was obviously aware that they were intending to take dinner with their client that night, but he had no way of knowing that they had been delayed in London.

Secondly, the inquest was told that, when he was arrested at Potash Farm, he protested, "That fellow Clarke has done this. It is he who has caused me to be suspected."

Of course, there is always the possibility that he intended to deal with all three of them at one fell swoop. It is a question which, one supposes, will never be answered.

As he recounted to me the story of the Rush murders, Bernard Gledhill made a great point of stressing the fact that a young employee of the firm, in his capacity as a special constable, was involved in the arrest of James Rush and the search of Potash Farm. That young man was Edward Boyce Pomeroy, a joiner's son from Exeter who, in 1845 and at the age of 17, had been taken on in the most humble position of clerk. Little did he, or anybody else, think that he and his family were destined to become major figures in the firm for more than a hundred years.

When he first joined the firm, Edward Pomeroy had no thought of becoming a solicitor but, as the years went by, he applied himself to the service of his employers and accumulated such knowledge of law practice that, in 1874, the Law Society passed him for qualification, at the ripe old age of 47.

Earlier, he had found himself a Norfolk wife in the shape of a certain Miss Bartle from Stibbard, and she duly presented him with a son, to whom they gave the names John Bartle. Hence were laid the foundations of the future firm, Pomeroy and Son.

By 1946 the younger Mr Pomeroy, having attained the age of 78, decided it was time to look around for a partner, and his choice fell upon Bernard Oliver Leathes Prior, a Norwich solicitor whose business had been in being for a lengthy period.

The following year brings us back to my friend and story-teller, Bernard Gledhill, for it was on January 7th 1947 that he joined the staff of Pomeroy and Son. Having returned from war service and qualified as a lawyer, he chuckled as he told me that one of the privileges offered to the newly-qualified, if they so wished, was the chance of receiving their certificates from the head of the Law Society, and afterwards of taking tea with him.

"And did you?" I asked.

"Indeed I did", he replied. "There's nothing like hobnobbing with the Top Brass!"

In 1951 Bernard was taken into partnership with B.H. and B.O. Leathes Prior and the firms came together as one.

The following year, John Bartle Pomeroy died, ending a century-old association between his family and the firm. In earlier years the name of the firm had changed with every new set of partners. On this occasion, however, the name lived on, for it was considered to be both well-known and highly regarded.

In 1958 the partnership was dissolved by mutual agreement and Bernard Gledhill purchased the ownership. New partners joined later, and in 1986 he decided to go into semi-retirement as consultant to the firm, handing over the reins to his nephew, David Pennell, to lead Pomeroy and Son towards the 21st century. This gave Bernard more time to delve into the past and uncover more stories to pass on to people like me.

Bernard Gledhill departed this life on Boxing Day, 1997. Since then, committee meetings have somehow never been quite the same.

INGWORTH MILL
(Demolished July 1913)

Good-bye, good-bye, old friend, good-bye, old mill,
One last farewell before they lay thee low;
A wreck? No! No! Thy former craft and skill
Needed no longer – therefore thou must go.

Nor shine, nor shade, on thy white walls shall fall,
Nor rising mists about thee curl and creep;
Vainly the breeze may seek, the rough wind call,
Or the lone river round thee fondly sweep.

No sound of splashing wheel, or clinking chain,
No footfall in the loft, or on the stair;
Gone the soft crunching of the grinding grain,
Only the lonely river weeping there.

Good-bye, good-bye, old mill! Thy work is done,
Like theirs who rest beside thee on the hill;*
Their labours ended, now thine hour is come,
No further need for thee, old Ingworth Mill!

Nay! Still we see thee in the empty air;
Naught can be quite effaced, nor good, nor ill;
And in our visions shall our spirits rear
Pale tender memories of Ingworth Mill.

M.J.K.

* The churchyard is on a knoll opposite the mill.

*The above lines appeared in the Eastern Daily Press,
July 16th, 1913.*

Ingworth Mill, with the Church looking down from a little hillock across the road.

133

CHAPTER 17

Brushes with the Famous

We were something of a mixed foursome, age-wise if not in other ways, as we sat chatting and sipping coffee in the shade of a walnut tree in Betty's garden. Betty herself was a child of the thirties, while dear old Tom first saw the light of day during the years of the previous world war, though his sparkling approach to life and his impeccable recall of times long past combined to belie his near-ninety years. As for me, well, I came somewhere in between while Jem, Betty's grandson, must have been hovering around the twenty mark.

It was Jem who introduced the topic of 'brushes with the famous' into our conversation, for he had been to a pop concert on the previous evening and it had obviously made a great impression on him. I have no recollection of the name of the singer in question, but he was one of those who have the charisma to draw young people in their thousands to an open arena to hear him perform, many so distant as to have the most minimal view of what is taking place on the stage. It was a memorable night for Jem, made even more so by the fact that, when it was all over, the object of his adulation actually walked away to his waiting car within just a few yards of Jem.

"He was so close," said Jem. "I could have touched him!"

We smiled indulgently, and then he turned to me and said, "But you've done much better than that, haven't you? You've shaken hands with Winston Churchill."

I had mentioned the incident in an earlier book, so either he had read about it or perhaps his grandmother had told him the story. It was at an event in Woodford, where we had been raising money for War Weapons Week, and I was in the process of counting our takings when the familiar figure appeared before me. He looked at the piles of pennies in front of me and asked how we had done.

"Very well, sir," I replied. "I make it just over fifty pounds."

"Well done, lad," he said, and it was at that moment that he extended his hand and grabbed mine with such vigour.

As we spoke, I glanced over his shoulder into the distance to where, some hundred or so yards away, there stood the car which had brought him, and in which sat the lone figure of his ever-patient driver. There had been no sudden arrival of support vehicles, no security men, as would now be considered necessary. There was no police presence. I doubt whether even the parish bobby was anywhere to be seen. There was just Winston Churchill – a man alone with his people. That was the mark of his greatness. And that is why I still recall that day with pride.

"But," said Jem when I had finished my story, "surely your fifty pounds wouldn't go far towards buying a Spitfire or a battleship."

"Quite true," I said, "but Britain was a very patriotic nation and, on that day, vast numbers of people right across the land had been doing exactly what we had been doing in Woodford. And," I added, "don't forget – we raised it all in single pennies."

I went on to explain that we had done it by getting members of the public to throw pennies into rubber rings just large enough to make it possible but sufficiently small to make sure it wouldn't happen too frequently. Furthermore, it was before decimalisation and they were old British pennies – and it took 240 of them to make a pound. That meant that our takings that day, even after paying out cash to successful contestants, totalled more than twelve thousand pennies – it sounds much better when you put it that way!

"Any more stories?" asked Jem.

"Well," I said, "I could tell you about the day I nearly head-butted the Archbishop of Canterbury."

"You nearly did what?" said the eager Jem.

It was in the mid-sixties, and we were on a family holiday in Canterbury. We were walking along the path outside the Cathedral precinct, deep in conversation, when I looked up and, to my consternation, I beheld the Archbishop coming towards me, directly on course for a head-on collision. I cannot recall which Archbishop it was, but he was a very well-known figure, instantly recognisable, and anyway he was clad in his vestments. Realising that quick action was necessary, I immediately stepped into the road to allow him to pass, but he, also aware of the situation, took similar action, and there we were, facing each other – the closest I have ever been to an Archbishop in my life. The great trouble, however, was that, when one suddenly stops going forward, the feet may stop dead, but the upper part of one's body tends to sway forward slightly. That was just what my body did, as also did that of the Archbishop, and I swear that, as our heads went forward in unison, they were for a split second barely more than a few inches apart.

I tried to cover my confusion by raising my arm to invite him to proceed along the path, and he immediately copied my action. But he had the advantage of me, for his face bore not only the most benign of smiles but also an expression of utter calmness and self-control. I whispered a quiet "Thank you, Your Grace" and accepted his invitation to proceed.

Then it was Tom's turn to regale us with memories of his University days at Cambridge, where, so soon after the end of the Great War, he remembered Admiral Beatty and Field Marshall Haig arriving to receive honorary degrees. Tom was in Downing Street to see them being 'chaired' from the Senate House to Emmanuel College, Beatty being carried by ex-sailors and Haig by ex-army men. Much has been written by more recent historians about Haig's alleged unpopularity with his soldiers. "But," said Tom, "none of it showed that day. Downing Street was solid with cheering, running men, to the exclusion of all traffic."

Then there was the day when he saw the young Crown Prince of Japan, later to become Emperor Hirohito, posing for an official photograph on the steps of Emmanuel College.

"I don't know what he made of it all," said Tom, "but he looked as scared as a rabbit. Little did we think that he was to be the Emperor who would later declare war on us and finally surrender to the country which was his host that day."

Probably Tom's most lasting memory of those days, however, was of two young men who took their places in the history of athletics and whose prowess was celebrated in the film *Chariots of Fire*. Their names were Abrahams and Burghley. Tom had never taken any great interest in sporting activities, but it was a very pleasant afternoon and, when a fellow-student asked for his company at an athletics event at Fenners in which his friend Burghley was running, Tom agreed to join him. Burghley was taking part in the hurdles race – "a very artificial sort of obstacle race," thought Tom – but first they made their way to the eastern side of the ground to see the sprinting.

They had no idea whatsoever that anything spectacular was about to take place; even Abrahams' closest associates showed no obvious sign of anticipation. For years there had been talk of man achieving a hundred-yards sprint in ten seconds, but all the experts said the human body was not capable of such a feat. Yet that was just what happened. When the time was actually broken, the significance of the fact was slow to sink in. Tom remembers little more than a polite handclap when Abrahams won, but, by the time they had walked over to the other part of the ground where the hurdle races were run, they began to realise that they had just witnessed a piece of history.

What they did not realise, however, was that, within minutes, Burghley was to break another world record in the hurdles – before their very eyes. This time, the excitement was intense as the crowd of onlookers literally jumped for joy – and that joy was reflected in old Tom's face as, all those years later, we sat in Betty's garden and listened to his tale of the day when two young men earned their places in Britain's sporting Hall of Fame.

It then fell to Betty to tell us of her 'brush with the famous,' and it proved to be not only the briefest but, by general acclaim, the most delightful of all the tales told that afternoon. Betty was the only one of the foursome who could not claim true Norfolk blood but, as she had been here for half a century since the day she took unto herself a Norfolk husband, she is happy to be 'one of us.' Her story, however, was of an incident during her childhood in Windsor, where her father was a gardener to the Royal Family.

She was about seven or eight years old at the time and was walking home from school when she suddenly realised that a large car had suddenly slowed down and stopped on the road beside her. She turned to look and, as the window opened, a very aristocratic-looking lady leaned forward and asked her if she would like a lift.

"Oh, no thanks," said Betty. "Mummy told me never to take lifts from people she doesn't know."

"But, my dear," said the aristocratic lady, "I'm Queen Mary."

"Yes, I know," replied Betty, "but Mummy doesn't know you."

Of course, most of my brushes with the famous in the world of entertainment came about during the eight years when I went 'on the wireless.' Two o'clock on a Tuesday was my usual slot, and that was also the afternoon when one of the stars from that week's presentation at the Theatre Royal would drop in to be interviewed. They came in great variety and, over the years, their names must surely have read like an Equity membership list.

I recall one particular lady, one of the most admired stars of the theatre (and rightly so) who needed no audience. Her entrance had to be seen to be believed. The manner in which she swept in through the front door of Norfolk Tower and on into Reception was worthy of, at least, a fanfare of trumpets, if not a 21-gun salute. Then there was the delicate way in which she declined the offer of BBC coffee in a paper cup with a mere lifting of one eyebrow that spoke volumes.

Then there was Anna Carteret, who kept her acting for the stage and offered her own natural self to the Radio Norfolk microphone. Seemingly untouched by the fame that she had acquired in so many television performances, she was as good at listening as at talking. Then, when she spoke, it was with a natural clarity of diction that was a joy to hear amidst today's plethora of untidy accents – and, every now and again, there was a smile which had 'sincerity' written all over it. Yes, I took quite a shine to Anna Carteret.

The person who most captivated me, however, was Donald Sinden, with whom I was fortunate to share a studio on three separate occasions. There are three things I always associate with Donald Sinden – a newspaper (always carries one), a packet of cigarettes (never without them) and that deep, smooth, chocolate-flavoured voice.

It was on the day of our first meeting that he divulged the secret of 'the voice.' Like so many other pillars of the stage, he had spent his early days as a young man in repertory, tackling a wide variety of parts as each one came along. One day, however, the director took him aside and told him that he had found a first class play which needed a strong romantic male lead on whom the impact of the plot largely depended. Donald, he said, had all the necessary attributes – except one. Believe it or not, his weakness was his voice, which, he said, was at that time 'a bit on the thin side.' Donald tried hard to deepen it, but to no avail, and it was decided that the only solution was to put him in the hands of a speech therapist. The thought of Donald Sinden needing the help of such a person now seems ludicrous, but the lady in question brought forth a miracle in training him to bring his voice up from much lower down in his body. Hence was born the voice which is now almost his trademark.

It was during that first meeting, also, that one of the 'girls' in Reception – I think it was Nancy – took a photograph of the pair of us. She gave me a copy and, when he came on the second

With Donald Sinden at Radio Norfolk.

occasion, I showed it to him and asked him to sign it for me. He obliged, and then said, "You don't happen to have a spare copy, do you?" I, of course, did not, but Nancy dived her hand into her bag and produced one.

"Splendid!" he said. "Now, dear boy, could I please ask you to sign this one for me?"

It was an uncanny feeling, and I am left with the image of some future biographer sorting through Donald's papers prior to writing his life story, finding the photograph and wondering who on earth is this chap 'Bob?'

During the period of Donald Sinden's first two visits to Radio Norfolk the anti-smoking crusade had not yet reached the stage of a ban inside Norfolk Tower, which suited him very nicely, for he enjoyed the peaceful puffing of a cigarette. By the time we shared the studio for the third time, however, the situation had changed completely, with smoking banned throughout the building – and that was when the sparks began to fly. I was already in the studio doing my party piece with Keith Skipper when the door opened and Nancy quietly ushered Donald in, one index finger held to her lips and the other pointing to the red light. He crept in as quietly as a mouse and sat down by my right hand side.

I kept going and then, out of the corner of my eye, I caught a glimpse of his hand going into his pocket and bringing out a packet of cigarettes. Then, out came his lighter and he took his first puff. There was nothing I could do to stop him, so I glanced across at Keith, whose face bore just the suggestion of a smile. It was then that Nancy came back into the studio with the obligatory BBC coffee in its paper cup and, seeing the cigarette smoke curling upwards, she exploded without making a sound. By that, I mean her face took on an expression of utter anger and she started frantically waving her arms about in a pretty fair impersonation of Magnus Pike. Donald got the message but could do no more than hold his hands out and look around the studio, for there were no longer any ash trays. Nancy immediately flew from the studio, only to return within about three seconds with a receptacle to receive the forbidden weed. She thrust it before him, but he was not to be rushed. Slowly and meticulously he squeezed the lighted end of the cigarette into her receptacle – and then replaced the unsmoked remainder back in its packet. Nancy, eyes cast up to the heavens, strode out with her trophy – and, all the while, I kept talking into the microphone and hoping that what I was saying made sense.

You know, that's the great disadvantage of radio – the listeners miss all the best bits!

Donald and I left the studio together at the end of the broadcast and, as we made our way through to Reception, I noticed that his once-lit cigarette was back in his hand. After an assurance that a taxi was organised to take him back to the Theatre Royal, he gave me a smile, glanced at the cigarette and said, "I think I might as well wait for it outside." I asked whether I might join him, and back came that deliciously chocolate-flavoured sound: "By all means, dear boy."

His taxi was a long time coming – to our mutual satisfaction, I think, for he seemed to derive as much pleasure from chuckling his way through a stream of anecdotes as I did from listening to the voice that had always fascinated me.

I told him that the first time I had seen him in action was in 1952, when he played the part of a young Naval Officer in *The Cruel Sea*. It was, in my view, one of the best Second World War films ever made, with a cast list packed with stars like Jack Hawkins, Stanley Baker, Denholm Elliot and Jack Warner.

"Don't remind me," he said. "Week after week soaked to the

skin and frozen to the marrow."

"Where did you film it?" I asked, thinking of the Mediterranean or somewhere similar.

"Pinewood," he said.

"But Pinewood is only a studio," I said. "Where did you do the location shots?"

"Pinewood, dear boy," he said. "The whole bally lot was shot at Pinewood – in the biggest metal tank I've ever seen – ten feet deep and as big as a soccer pitch. And it was full to the brim with the coldest water in Christendom. And, to be perfectly honest, I was never much of a swimmer."

Then he told me of the occasion when, with the day's filming completed, the director decided to take advantage of the actors' already waterlogged condition in order to acquire some footage of each of the men swimming away from their sinking ship. The camera was to focus on one particular stretch of water and would continue to roll as each of the four successively swam into shot and out again. Then, when the time came to edit the film, the individual shots could be inserted at the appropriate points in the action.

The camera duly rolled and the action took place, with Donald Sinden the third one to move across the scene. When the resulting shot was examined, however, something was missing. Jack Hawkins was there alright, followed a short while later by Stanley Baker, but then came a longer gap before Denholm Elliot came into view. There was no sign of Donald Sinden. He assured the director that he was there, but he could do no more than shamefacedly admit that he was swimming in the only way he could – underwater breast-stroke.

A re-take was ordered, but once again Donald could not be seen!

The director, however, was not a man to accept defeat lightly. Desperate situations call for desperate measures, and he immediately sent for a stunt man in the form of a certain Frankie Howard – though not, I hasten to add, the bearer of that name who later achieved fame with his camp humour! The idea was that he should do the sub-aqua breast-stroke and, at the same time, provide support for Donald as he struck out from the ship in a manner more befitting a Naval Officer. The resulting sequence appeared most authentic when the film was eventually completed – little did the paying public realise that Donald Sinden was being carried across the screen on Frankie Howard's back.

At that moment, his taxi put in an appearance, but he hurriedly wanted to tell me something else before he left.

"I owe my life to Jack Hawkins," he said.

It seems that one day, after filming, the men had made a rapid exit in search of a hot bath and warm clothing when somebody suddenly shouted, "Where's Donald?" Jack Hawkins took to his heels and sprinted back to the tank, and there, in the distance, were the rising air bubbles marking Donald's position in the water. Being unable to keep his head above the surface, he was never quite sure he was going in the right direction. He was already near exhaustion when they hauled him out.

"Yes," he said, "he saved my life, did Jack Hawkins."

There was a wave of his newspaper, the taxi door was closed, and away he went, off to face another audience.

CHAPTER 18

The Hundred Thousand Dollar Wager

The world is full of mysteries, and I am not averse to them – as long as there is some way of solving them. Crossword puzzles in newspapers are acceptable for, even if there is the occasional clue which defies one's efforts at decoding, it is only necessary to wait for the next day's issue of the paper and all will be revealed. It is the same with detective and murder mysteries, where the writer tends to take readers along a multitude of side turnings and cul-de-sacs in order to throw suspicion in the direction of as many of the characters as possible. Yet, once again, the solution is there. One only has to patiently wade through the many pages of red herrings – or better still, have a crafty peep at the last page – and one will know whether it really was the butler who did it!

There is, however, a mystery which has bothered me for a long time, and I am no nearer solving it than I was on the day when I first heard of it.

The story begins on a day in 1907 when a certain well-known – though unidentified – American millionaire became involved in a heated argument in a Gentlemen's Club in the Pall Mall area of London. The cause of the disagreement was his stated belief that no Englishman was capable of walking round the world wearing a mask and pushing a perambulator. So firm was his belief that he was prepared to wager the sum of a hundred thousand dollars (the equivalent of £21,000 in English currency) to anybody who could prove him wrong, subject to certain conditions which he, himself, would impose. These conditions included the stipulation that the challenger should remain masked and entirely unknown throughout the entire journey and that all expenses of the journey should be defrayed by the sale of photographs and pamphlets. The challenger would be "allowed to expend any sum not exceeding One Pound (£1) for Photographs and Pamphlets for sale at the start," and would be allowed to continue selling them while on the journey.

At this point I feel I should reveal that, somewhat surprisingly, a mystery man accepted the challenge and proceeded to obtain a

Walking Round The World . . .

MASKED,

Pushing a Perambulator.

100,000 DOLLAR
Wager.

THE LARGEST WAGER ON RECORD.

Full Conditions of this Wager, and the Route to be taken, will be found in this Pamphlet.

D. JACKSON, Printer 212, Whitehorse Lane, South Norwood, S.E.

144

supply of publicity material, the sale of which would finance his journey. I have in my keeping at the present time a photograph of the masked man and a copy of the pamphlet in which he described the task which lay ahead. Far better, I feel, to let him take up the story.

"After hearing the conditions," he wrote, "I at once made up my mind to accept the wager. Upon telling him the decision I had come to, he at once made arrangements with another well-known American gentleman, who has kindly consented to hold the stakes. As will be seen by the Conditions, I am on no account to reveal my identity during the whole journey.

"With reference to Condition number 12, it will be seen that I am to find a Wife whilst on the journey. She must be between the age of 25 and 30, well-educated, of even temper, with some knowledge of music."

Then, in bold type, he added:

"This Condition has been complied with."

He then went on to list the remaining conditions, as follows:

> To start from Trafalgar Square, London, on the 1st day of January, 1908, at 10-30 a.m. *sharp.*
>
> To call at the capital city and three other towns named in the appended list, in each County in England.
>
> To obtain a document, signed by the Mayor, or any responsible person, certifying that you arrived at the place mentioned therein and the date thereof.
>
> To obtain the Postal Stamp of every Town passed through on your journey.
>
> The wearing apparel to be worn at the start to consist of the following articles:-
>
> One suit of clothes, one pair of stockings, one shirt, one undervest, one pair pants, one pair boots, one pair of putties, one jersey, one handkerchief, one mask.

Thus would begin his trek around Britain, masked and pushing his perambulator. The counties had to be visited in a specific order, beginning with Kent and visits to Maidstone, Woolwich, Chatham and Dover. From there he was to work his way along the coastal counties to Cornwall, after which he would turn and make his way eastwards along the adjoining counties from Somerset to Essex. Then it was Suffolk's turn to see him, followed by Norfolk, with visits to Norwich, Thetford, Yarmouth and King's Lynn.

Then, by trekking back and forth across the country, he would find himself in Northumberland, after which came a trip over the border to Edinburgh, Stirling, Glasgow and Greenock, and an over-the-water visit to Belfast, Dundalk, Dublin and Cork.

By that time, he would have covered 43 counties and visited 172 towns and cities. It was, admittedly, an arduous task, but surely not beyond a man with sufficient dedication and will-power, especially bearing in mind the fact that there appears to have been no set time limit. He could have rested when necessary – and, no doubt, got busy selling his photographs and pamphlets.

But, of course, it was, in reality, the easy part of the wager – what the showjumping fraternity might have called the Practice Fence. Ahead of him lay the international part of his task, and the mere thought of his destinations conjures up alarming images, especially in an age when foreign travel was not the everyday activity it has now become.

The conditions of the wager decreed that he was to visit the Countries of the World in the following order:-

England, Scotland, Ireland, Canada, United States of America, South America, New Zealand, Australia, South Africa, Japan, China, India, Egypt, Italy, France, Spain, Portugal, Belgium, Germany and Holland.

The sobering thought is that, if he was to succeed and claim the reward, it would involve visiting twenty countries and no fewer than 292 towns and cities.

So, the burning question is – did he satisfy all the conditions and come back to live a life of luxury for the rest of his days? It is with much regret, and an even greater feeling of annoyance, that I have to confess to being unable to answer that question. It is just another wretched unsolvable mystery!

There are, I believe, four possible solutions. Firstly, he may have succeeded and then, perhaps, gone off to live in one of the high society resorts in the south of France, though I give this little credence. Then, of course, he may have tried and failed. Rather more likely, perhaps, but I am far from convinced. Thirdly, the whole affair may have been a practical joke but, if such was the case, why should he have gone to such lengths, and who was the intended butt of the joke?

Finally, we come to the solution which I personally favour. I would stress that I am not normally of a suspicious disposition, but it is my belief that the whole thing was nothing less than a cunningly-contrived confidence trick played on the British public.

Firstly, I cannot accept that anybody could have completed the overseas part of the wager, even though there was no time limit. Furthermore, the concept of supporting himself throughout the journey solely by selling photographs and pamphlets seems highly questionable. It might have been feasible in English-speaking countries, but I cannot visualise queues of customers in such places as Tokyo and Yokohama, Peking and Shanghai, or Delhi and Bombay.

It is the question of finance that lies at the heart of the matter, and I have much doubt as to whether there really was a wager in the first place. I believe it to be a cleverly concocted scheme which allowed him to turn up at country fairs and markets anywhere in Britain and sell his pamphlets and photos. He had all the time in the world, and there was much profit to be made.

Then there are certain strange conditions which were imposed. Why, for instance, should the American millionaire have stipulated that he should push a perambulator throughout his journey? Rather more likely, I feel, that this clause was inserted by the mystery man himself. After all, what better method could he have had to carry his stock of literature from place to place?

There is also the condition that, on his journey, he should find himself a wife who "must be between the age of 25 and 30, well-educated, of even temper, with some knowledge of music." Furthermore, there is the fact that, in his pamphlet produced *before* he started his trip, he stated that "this condition has been complied with." Much more likely, I suspect, that he already had such a wife.

Finally, there is the question of the mask and the insistence that he should, at all times on the journey, "maintain his anonymity whilst walking and in all public places." If, at any time, his nefarious activity was revealed, what better way could he have had of ensuring that no suspicion would fall on him?

I suspect that there never was an American millionaire and certainly no hundred thousand dollar wager. My suspicion is that the mystery man concocted the whole thing. But suspicion is not proof, and I fear that the answer to the mystery will never be revealed.

Much better, I feel, for me to content myself with crossword puzzles!

148

CHAPTER 19

As Others See Us

Over the years much has been made of the hesitancy of Norfolk folk to welcome strangers into their midst. Some would claim it to be merely a myth, but that is not so. It is part of our make-up - and for a very good reason.

It is all a matter of history for, over many centuries, the county has been taken over by invaders who, whilst admittedly bringing certain improvements, were determined to conquer our ancestors. There were the Romans, and just think what trouble they caused. The Normans came and, though they left us some fine buildings, their great aim was domination. Then there were the Saxons, more gentle and less war-like, to whom we should be eternally grateful for changing the very face of the Norfolk countryside. Finally came the Vikings, bringing with them their national sport of rape and pillage and the urge to win at all costs.

All those invaders must have had their effect on the Norfolk countryman, and I have a vision of him quietly going about his business and continually looking back over his shoulder lest an unknown stranger might be in the offing. Is it any wonder, then, that we are loath to fling our arms wide to welcome the first sight of newcomers? Is it not understandable that we should wish to "summer an' winter em fust?"

One man who learned to love the countryfolk of Norfolk was Canon W. H. Marcon, the much-loved and still well-remembered Rector of Edgefield from 1876 to 1937.

He was, in fact, a Norfolk man by birth, having been born in the very parish, on the outskirts of Holt, where he was later to tend his flock. In his early life, however, he knew little of the ordinary Norfolk folk and their ways, for he was educated in Devon until he reached the age of fifteen. During the next four years, he and his brother joined the Norfolk Imperial Yeomanry, into which they threw themselves with great enthusiasm, walking to and fro to drill at Holt. He remembered being measured for 'a grey suit with braided border,' and he also recalled the occasion when, together with others from various parts of Norfolk, the Holt Corps went into camp at Hunstanton Park, where they gained the name of the 'Glorious XIXth' because they made more noise than any other corps.

By the time he was 19, his great uncle, a don at Magdalen College, Oxford, was putting pressure upon him to go to University and work for a degree with a view to entering the priesthood. This he did, receiving his degree at the age of 22. It was then to be another year before he could be ordained, so he filled the interval by taking up a couple of tutorships for sons of members of the landed gentry. His first pupil was the son of Lady Downe, of Baldersby in Yorkshire.

"A tutor's life in such a house," he wrote, "is rather lonely; he is between the drawing room and the servants' hall, belonging to neither. But I saw a little of the hunting in Yorkshire, and fishing on the Tweed."

He left this position to take up another tutorship, this time for two sons of Sir Edward Strachey, one of whom was destined to become the proprietor and editor of *The Spectator.*

"Thus," he wrote, "I was brought into the atmosphere of cultured minds."

When the time came for him to find a curacy, it was at Govillon, near Abergavenny. There, among the Welsh quarrymen and colliers, he worked for two years until the death of his father called him home and he was offered the living of Edgefield. He found himself, at the age of 25, still lacking in experience, called upon to undertake a task full of hidden difficulties.

"Goodbye, ye happy carefree days of boyhood," he wrote. "Goodbye, ye sweet mixture of work and play, and all the intercourse of College life at Oxford. I shall never more taste your exuberance of health and spirit. They come but once in a lifetime and must give way to the calls of serious duties."

Then comes the confession, written in 1933:

"My impressions of country folk may here be stated for the sake of others in like position. Coming as a young man from a large curacy in the West of England and not so long after the sweet camaraderie of College life - so full of animation and vigorous thought - I found life amongst bucolics very slow and lonely. I thought them ignorant, inexperienced, and wished I could transplant them for six months into the Midlands, where a daily newspaper was a common thing, and then bring them back again.

But I have corrected and abandoned this view. Ignorant they certainly are not, but very full of knowledge of such things as they were familiar with and I was not.

"I came to see and to learn that a farm hand, occupied as he is in a widely varied work from January 1st to December 31st, must have a correspondingly wide knowledge, with the skill and brain and hand that will class him amongst the skilled workers of the world. To manage the plough at the *end* of the furrow as well as along it, to know the various parts, to drill the corn *straight,* to set out and build a stack in such a way that it shall stand and keep out the rain, to know his cattle and the signs of anything wrong. And when machinery goes wrong, how often he 'twigs' where the fault is, and can put it right.

"No, I found myself looking up to men who knew so much. They might not be able to read a book, but they could read a field."

J. B. Priestley came and 'wrote us up' in 1933, but he came as a friend, having been here on a number of occasions and having enjoyed a number of friendships with the locals, particularly R. H. Mottram.

"I always find myself happy and at home" he wrote, " in the cities where I am asked at once, confidently and proudly, what I think of the place - and of course Norwich is one of those cities. Norwich is no mere provincial town; it is not simply an old cathedral city; it is something more - an antique metropolis, the capital of East Anglia. To thousands and thousands of good sensible folk who live and work there, Norwich is the big city, the centre, and has been these hundreds of years. It is no mere jumped-up conglomeration of factories, warehouses and dormitories. It is not filled with people who are there because they have never been offered a job elsewhere. No, Norwich is really a capital, the capital of East Anglia.

"As for the East Anglian," he wrote, "he is a solid man. Lots of beef and beer, tempered with east wind, have gone to the making of him. Once he is sure you are not going to cheat him or be very grand or affected, he is a friendly chap; but if you want the other thing, you can have it. The Ironsides were recruited from these parts, which have produced a great many fighting men of all kinds, from pugilists to admirals."

One evening, Priestley and Mottram dined together at the

Maid's Head before going to see *The School for Scandal* at the Maddermarket Theatre.

"How delightful," he wrote, "to turn in from dusky old St Andrew's Street and St. John's Alley and find oneself at Lady Sneerwell's. How delightful when the piece was done and Nugent Monck had been congratulated, to wander out again into the ancient streets, where at every corner a bit of lamplight revealed century after century in a gable, a bit of heavily shadowed timbering or a bulging bay window. Delightful, too, to have a last drink, sprawling in front of the fire at the Maid's Head, and to hear the honest roars of a Norfolk man as he describes to you his bemused adventures in certain artistic quarters of that remote and fantastic fellow capital city, London."

In 1935 Norfolk received a visit from the 'broadcasting farmer', A. G. Street, who described himself as 'merely a humble tenant farmer, owning not a single square foot of land.' He had been born at Ditchampton Farm in the county of Wiltshire in 1892 and, after his father's death, he had taken over the tenancy in his own right from Michaelmas, 1918.

When he was in his fifties, he calculated that he and his father had paid out in annual rents to their landlord several times the freehold value of the holding. "And yet." he wrote, "I am not one penny nearer owning it that when my father began the business."

But A. G. Street was a proud man - a 'Moonraker,' a Wiltshireman born and bred, and he readily confessed to having a lifetime love affair with the land he worked.

"It is queer," he said, "how love for land, especially love for a farm, gets hold of a man. In most cases, certainly in mine, it transcends all other loves - love of women, love of children, love of friends, love of animals, love of country, everything. Which is, perhaps, a shameful admission, but a true one."

So it was that, in 1935, he paid what I believe to be his only visit to Norfolk. The trouble was that he came with a host of pre-conceived misconceptions and a wagonload of bias. The invitation had come from farming friends in north-west Norfolk, and his Wiltshire friends said that, if he 'accepted the dare,' he would be lucky if he returned home 'with a whole skin!'

From the conversation at the dinner table on the first evening he gathered that his great crime against Norfolk was that he, a mere Southerner, had dared to criticise our county in any way.

"Apparently," he wrote, "Norfolk is beyond criticism, and my hosts did their best during my stay to show me the error of my ways. They did more - they invited their many friends to lunch and dinner and tea in order that they might help in the good work, and they took me by car and on foot over acres and acres of Norfolk's farming."

In one respect, they failed to change his views about Norfolk, and that was its comparative isolation from the traffic of the nation.

"The main route from north to south, either by road or rail, misses it completely," he wrote, "and, apart from the sugar-beet industry, factories are few and far between. Norfolk is a farming county. There one talks farming, thinks farming, dreams farming and lives farming almost to the exclusion of all else. And change - any change - even a change for the better - is regretted. Another impression I gathered during my stay was that Norfolk's farming community does not approve of interlopers from other parts of the country. One has to be born and bred in Norfolk to fit in properly, and I should imagine it would take at least three generations before one ever belonged. All crimes, troubles and sins both of omission and commission are traced to the alien farmer, and I hope for his sake that nobody will perpetrate a trunk murder in Norfolk. If this should occur, everybody in the district would point to the nearest interloper as the culprit, and a Norfolk jury would hang him out of hand."

Then, however, completely without warning, there came signs that he was beginning to mellow:

"But what a lovely unspoilt land Norfolk is! Modern civilisation, with its hustle and bustle and noise, seems to have passed it by. Buses are comparatively few and far between; cars seem to recognise that other people, even walking with three or four puppies, have a right to the road; a serene peace seems to brood over the countryside; and everybody, from the squire downwards, has a genuine love for the land.

"To travel is to learn, and one result of my visit is that now I have a better knowledge of Norfolk's difficulties and a much higher opinion of Norfolk's countryside and its dwellers. Also I am daring to hope that some of them may say that the interloper for one most enjoyable and friendly week-end was not as bad as he had been painted."

Finally, a report published in *The Eastern Daily Press* on April 25th, 1939. Less than a lifetime ago, but now surely of little more than historical interest:

The banquet of the London Society of East Anglians, at which the easterlings in London meet annually to sing to one another the praises of their native counties, was chiefly remarkable this year for suggestions that we might do well, if we wish to keep the charm of this eastern district - still little known to the mob in motor cars - to sing its praises softly and only to ourselves.

First we had the Duke of Grafton attributing an unspoilt countryside to the blessing of a bad railway service, which deters people from coming here; and then the Bishop of St. Edmundsbury and Ipswich saying that although there has been much reference of late to the charm of the countryside in Suffolk, this does not mean that we want people to come building bungalows and turning quiet country lanes into by-pass roads with rushing cars.

Our detractors may say that here is proof from ducal and episcopal lips that the East Anglian defect of insularity and coldness to strangers pervades the whole population, from the highest to the lowest. Yet, may there not be some wisdom in this advice that, still being blessed with some quiet countryside, we should keep it quiet?

A distinguished man came recently from Devonshire - yes, Devonshire - to live in North Norfolk, declaring that here was one of the last vestiges of the real rural England as he conceived it. Are we to be blamed for cherishing such quietude a little jealously?

154

5

The Royal Cooper Story

THE ROYAL COOPER STORY

I – The Early Years

I readily confess to a lifetime addiction to books. What is more, I have long known this addiction to be completely incurable, and the sight of a well-stocked second-hand bookshop unfailingly draws me to it like a magnet. Even so, I would have it no other way, for my love of other people's writing has taken me into the very lives of those people, most of whom I would probably never have known.

Visits to bookshops can sometimes be very brief, as, for instance, when one tries to track down a certain volume. Much more enjoyable, however, is the 'browse', when the passage of time is of no consequence and one can take a leisurely look along the shelves in the hope that there is something that might take one's fancy. I well remember the occasion on which I held one such book in my hands and wondered whether I should turn from 'browser' to 'purchaser'.

It was a slim, unpretentious little volume, bound in blue and bearing the inscription "Poems and Proverbs by Royal W.J. Cooper." I had never heard of the book and knew nothing of the author but, as I casually glanced at the flyleaf at the front of the book, my mind was made up for me, for it was there that a previous owner had written these words:

The author, a Norfolk farmer, was incarcerated in Thorpe Asylum for nearly six years in the thirties for non-payment of tithes.

The die was cast. I had to have it. I paid the bookseller his asking price of £1.95 and set off to seek out the Royal Cooper Story.

As luck would have it, I was committed to doing a broadcast from Norwich a few days later, and Radio Norfolk listeners are renowned for their eagerness to help with matters of this nature, so I slipped in a brief mention of my quest. The result was quite amazing, for phone calls started coming in even before the broadcast had finished, and letters and messages continued arriving for several weeks. I began to think that I was the only

Royal Cooper in mid-life.

person in Norfolk who had never known Royal Cooper!

Most significantly, the constant factor which shone through all the messages that came in was the high regard in which he was held by all who knew him. Born a Primitive Methodist, he was a man of high religious principles, a great believer in the virtue of hard work and a man with a great love for his fellow men. Furthermore, he was never known to utter a swear word, and he would never smack any of his children – yet each and every one turned out to be a credit to him. His forbearance as regards chastisement of his children is, perhaps, worthy of special praise for, even if he had done nothing else in his life, he and his wife Olive had founded a splendid dynasty, bringing a total of fourteen young Coopers into the world, with no bias towards either sex – there were seven of each! I can personally vouch for the kind of adults they grew to be, for I was soon to meet many of them on my visits, firstly to Bawdeswell, then to Themelthorpe, where Royal's eldest surviving son Jack was living with his wife Etta.

They were fascinating visits, with so many photographs and mementoes of Royal to be inspected and so many questions to be asked and answered. Eventually Jack said, "You know, Bob, you must have so many questions you want to ask, the best way to get your answers is to take this home and have a look through it" and, bending down behind the settee, he produced a very large suitcase, proudly displaying the initials R.J.W.C. He opened it and revealed a massive assortment of papers, letters, proofs of the man's poems, and documents in great variety. They were to occupy many hours of my time in the ensuing weeks.

Now, having perused so many hundreds of pages of his writings, I am impressed by a number of striking characteristics which they exhibit. Firstly there is my wonderment at the sheer beauty of his copper plate writing, surely the result of extremely lengthy practice. Then there is one little idiosyncracy which makes his writing unique, for, if all his writing was like the large quantity in his case, then it is a pretty safe assumption that he went through life without crossing a single t. Then there is the content of his writing – the fruits of a busy mind – a very enquiring mind. "All my life," he writes, "I have liked to get to the bottom of things," and I think it was that, together with more than a touch of Norfolk cussedness, that tended to bring him into conflict with the Establishment.

Royal William James Cooper was born on August 10th 1880 at Yew Tree Farm, Themelthorpe, one of a family of two brothers and six sisters. I suppose, by the standard of those times, it was a small family, but it might possibly have been larger had it not been for the fact that, when Royal was just six years old, his mother died while bringing a little girl into the world, leaving his aunt to play quite a part in his upbringing.

Later on, when he was in the mental hospital, he produced 40 pages of script which is headed "My Life Drama" and tells his life story. I started reading it, but found progress difficult, for it was not in his normal style. I had several attempts and then I suddenly realised that it was written in the form of a film script and, not only that, but he had even selected the young child he wanted to play himself as a boy:

Scene 1. Home and farm scene. My mother, my son Eric representing me; and Eric is shown holding his mother's skirt as she is about her work.

Scene 2. Showing the funeral of my mother – coffin leaving the homestead and passing to church.

Scene 3. Schoolhood days. John (my elder brother) with donkey and cart driving 5 children to school. Children at desks and in the school playground.

Then a scene with a pond covered with ice, which breaks and lets me in. I go back to school wearing my wet trousers. I say nothing about it, but one of the boys tells the master, who orders me off home. On the way home I find an old newspaper, take off my trousers and try to wipe them dry. On arriving home I get a scolding from my father.

My brother and I are now seen with a donkey, pulling a sledge on snow. To make it more exciting we drive by the edge of the ditch and turn over. We do this several times until I get my arm broken. We return home with the result, and my brother is sent off on the donkey's back to fetch the doctor...

Approaching adulthood. I am now at work at home doing a bit of dealing and saving what I can. I have rather high ideas and believe honest labour is a sure way to success. Having saved about £80 and my brother just about £40, we take a little farm at Guestwick. It had been badly let down. We worked hard on our own farm and the Home Farm for our father. We had a small flock of ewes at one time and when lambing time came I decided to stay at the farm. I made a bed of sacks and straw in a bullock shed,

160

my brother staying with me on the first night – that was enough for him and he didn't stop any more.

Later we left the farm and took another one at Bawdeswell, Mr Francis Hornor being the agent for Evans Lombe Esquire. The farm was heavy land in bad condition. The valuer, having completed his task, just leaving the farm in his gig, shook my hand, saying, "I wish you the best of luck, but you'll be a long while making a fortune here."

We worked hard from early morn till late at night, walking to and from our home at Themelthorpe for the first year. We then lived at the farm, a sister keeping house for us. Eventually we left the farm and had a sale at which we realised some good prices, and then we dissolved the partnership.

Later in his narrative comes a delightful story of a trip he made to London somewhere around the year 1910, when he was about thirty, for the purpose of buying a couple of horses from the Barbican Repository. He was always a great horseman, and I am told that, later on, at harvest time, he always had eight Suffolks working in the fields – surely a grand sight! He also had a Clydesdale which rather disgraced itself on one occasion by kicking poor old Bob Dyball. Bob Dyball worked for Royal for twenty years or so and, as was Royal's custom, when Bob retired, Royal wrote a poem to mark the occasion. It ran to about thirty verses, and in it he recorded Bob's kick:

I once bought a mare at a Yarmouth sale;
I've no doubt Bob Dyball could tell you the tale.
He was taking her harness off just past her rib
When she kicked poor Bob Robert right under the crib.
Perhaps Bob would tell you where he would be now
If her heel had a-hit him on the place where he chow.
He would not now be standing, but perhaps lying down
In a nice little box up at Swannington Town.

But we must return to his trip to London to get those two horses, which he described as "a big Shire and a heavy vanner." Having bought them, he made the brave, if not foolhardy, decision to walk them home from London. Hence, he set off, but the going was rather slow and night had fallen by the time he had got to Barking, which was not very far along the road. There, he was apprehended by the police, who suspected that he had come by the horses by some nefarious means, but he was able to reassure them by showing them receipts and cheque counterfoils. Then, a bit further on, he was accosted by a man who queried his wisdom in roaming the streets at that time of night.

"I assured him that I was alright," says Royal, "and, putting my hand to my breast pocket, I said, 'I have company here!' "

When I first read that passage I thought he was implying that he had a gun in his pocket, but, knowing the man as I now do, I feel sure he was signifying that he had God in his heart.

By the end of the next day he had got almost as far as Chelmsford, but both he and the horses were approaching a state of utter exhaustion, so he managed to get them on board a train to complete the remainder of the journey. Even then, however, it was still a matter of having to walk them from Norwich to Themelthorpe – a man of sturdy character indeed!

One aspect of his life story which I found quite amusing was the way in which he goes into great detail about his farming activities, yet domestic matters give the impression of being fitted into the narrative when he happens to think of them. Thus, we come to the following:

"I was now busy buying stock and implements for the farm I had hired at Themelthorpe through Messrs. Irelands. With hard work and care I managed to get along fairly well. Nothing unusual was happening, except that I was now keeping company with a girl 13 years my junior, much to the annoyance of my family. We were married in the year --- (and there is a blank which suggests he had forgotten which year it was, but it was, in fact, 1913) at the Registry Office at Aylsham, returning home to an empty house, my sister having taken flight after making the place nice and clean for our arrival."

At this point in his narrative he has arrived at the bottom of the page and suddenly realises that he has not told us the identity of the girl he has married. Hence, down the side of the page he has written "Olive Gaff of Bawdeswell, a small farmer's daughter."

"We settled down with plenty of work to do and little recreation. On May 28th --- (another blank, but it was 1914) our first daughter was born, being named Olive Irene. We kept several fowls, which the wife looked after, at times when not engaged with the bringing forth of young. Our second child, a son, was born on --- (another blank.)"

He then relates a variety of anecdotes, including the occasion when he went to Dereham just after the Zeppelin attack and found everybody white-faced with shock. Eventually the War ended and

162

his brother returned home to take over the Home Farm.

Many stories follow, including the occasion when he bought "various items of food-production machinery at a sale at Bury, including a Titan tractor and cultivator" – with which, it seems, he nearly killed himself. He apparently tried to open a gate while driving this tractor and cultivator without getting off and, somehow slipping between the two, he got caught. Luckily, he was able to lean over and slap the vehicle into reverse gear, at which point he made his escape.

Then, having received notice from his landlord that the rent for the farm was to be raised, he decided to terminate his tenancy and seek his fortune elsewhere. As luck would have it, a farm of 181 acres at Swannington then came up for sale, and he bought it. It was Jowles Farm, which he renamed *Woodlands,* and it was there that most of his children were born. It was there, also, that an unknown destiny lay in wait for him.

II – Woodlands

The year was 1921, and it ushered in a period of great significance to Royal Cooper and his burgeoning family. It was a period which was to see Woodlands become their own Home Farm, but which would also bring with it such extremes of joy and sorrow, happiness and despair as can have been the lot of very few families.

All the household goods and farming equipment made the journey to Swannington in the farm wagons and carts, while Mother drove the children over in their pony trap. Daughter İrene, then seven years old and the eldest child, later described it as "by far the longest journey we'd ever had," which, at barely ten miles, at first seems surprising, though it may be·that the condition of the roads may have made the journey seem longer than it really was. Tarmacadam had not yet penetrated to the byroads of Norfolk, and the only upkeep came at the hands of the parish lengthman, working with the heaps of stones and sand deposited by the Council at strategic points.

The last mile or so of their journey was the worst, for it took them along an unmade-up track with three farm gates to negotiate. The meadows through which they passed belonged to another farm; it was only when they closed the third gate behind them that they had entered their own territory and found the house

Woodlands Farm.

confronting them.

"It was much bigger than our old one," said Irene. "The walls were very high, one room was very grand with an ornate ceiling, a picture rail and a marble fireplace. All the windows had inside wooden shutters to keep out the cold on windy nights, for it was in a very exposed position.

"There were three living rooms, grandly called the dining room, the drawing room and the sitting room; also a very big kitchen-cum-dairy, a large walk-in pantry and a boxroom in which all our clean linen was kept. There was also a large cellar, and a green baize-covered door which separated the front of the house from the servants' quarters (we just had a girl from the village, and she lived with us). There were two staircases, and five bedrooms and a boxroom upstairs."

Irene, it seems, was suitably impressed.

The state of the road meant that very few delivery men called, the only regular exception being the long-suffering postman, for Royal always had his daily paper sent by post. The butcher came once a week until one day when he accidentally turned his van over into the horse pond. They managed to drag it out and rescue most of its cargo, but pots of brawn were still coming to the surface a fortnight later. Twice a week, one of the girls was sent to the baker in the village for three loaves of bread, but Mother always kept a 10-stone sack of flour in the bin and made six loaves twice a week. Mother used to drive to Reepham with the pony and tub cart each Wednesday, market day, to do her grocery shopping, and Father often went, usually with sheep, cattle or pigs to sell or buy at auction, or corn to trade with the merchants.

Everything in the household seems to have been done in a set routine which nothing seemed to change. Sunday breakfast there was always pheasant, partridge or rabbit pie, if in season, or else meat patties or sausage rolls. Weekday mornings it was always porridge, made in a double boiler saucepan using coarse ground oatmeal. Friday was always the main baking day, so Thursday afternoon would see Mother and 'the girl' either peeling apples and preparing other fruit for pies, or plucking game and cleaning rabbits for the same purpose.

But, all the time, Olive Cooper seemingly allowed nothing to divert her from her most regular activity – that of child-bearing. Every eighteen months, on average, a new member would join the family, with the result that, when the fourteenth finally arrived, there was a span of just over 21 years between first and last.

Meanwhile, Royal battled on against the odds to fulfil his duty, not only to his family, but also to his men – and when conditions were bad, it was the men's pay which had to be found first. In those days, even a fair-weather harvest took weeks to bring in, and a wet one went on much longer, with the men having to continually turn the sheaves in the stooks to prevent the corn from sprouting. Yet the workmen had to have their money, whatever the conditions, so that their children could have new clothes, while Royal's family had to wait until the corn had been threshed and sold.

Much of the land which Royal was now working was light and sandy – exactly the opposite of what he had been familiar with at Themelthorpe. He viewed this situation with mixed feelings, depending upon the season and weather conditions. His exposed situation meant that a spell of dry windy weather in Spring, after the sugar beet had been drilled, would send a cloud of sand billowing across the land, taking his beet seed with it. No alternative, then, but to buy more seed and drill all over again, something he could ill afford with even more mouths to feed and workmen to pay.

But there was another side to the situation, for it was the kind of grassy habitat so beloved by rabbits, and they were there in vast numbers. This pleased Royal, for he was handy with a gun and knew that his family would never go short of a meal.

Then there was harvest time, with horses and binders winding their almost leisurely way round the standing corn and gradually reducing the size of the last little area in the middle of the field. Nobody knows how the word got round, but it seemed as if all the able-bodied men of the village, armed with sticks to run the rabbits, would suddenly converge on the field. It was quite commonplace for anything from fifty to a hundred rabbits to be taken in one field alone, and everybody went home with at least one or two. Indeed, if Royal knew of anybody who had been unable to get there, he would send them a brace.

"Throughout the weeks of corn-cutting," said Irene, "the entire village must have smelt of rabbit pie, or rabbit stew or rabbit something-or-other."

It was an age when the horse was king in the countryside, and Royal was justly proud of the fine specimens which uncomplainingly went about their duties over his acres. He loved

Royal's horseman, Billy Green, with Culpho Mobility.

his horses, and he lavished more care and attention on them than he would ever have given to a tractor. They were almost invariably Suffolks, and there was one among their number which stood out from all the others in his affections. He was a Suffolk stallion, a magnificent creature with the equally splendid name of 'Culpho Mobility'. He had a stable to himself and was not expected to work like all the others – but he was taken for 'walks.' He was, indeed, a Show specimen, and Royal's horseman, Billy Green, took a great pride in grooming him and braiding his mane and tail. Then, every year, he would take him to the Norfolk Show and stay at the ground with him until he had taken his place in the judging ring. Sadly, he never achieved more than a 'Highly Commended,' but competition was strong, and Royal's chest would swell with pride as his stallion paraded in the ring with the best the county could offer.

Royal Cooper was a man of strongly-held principles, and he made sure that his family were not only aware of them but that they also abided by them. The girls were encouraged to engage in needlework, but only on weekdays. They were not allowed to do any knitting or sewing on a Sunday, nor could they play Snakes and Ladders or any of the other games they played during the week. And two things which were never allowed in the house, even on weekdays, were alcohol and playing cards – "the ruination of the Country and of many young men," he said.

For such a strict Methodist family, of course, it was inevitable that Sundays were dominated by the demands of the Chapel. The Sunday School was largely in the hands of two of the three sisters who ran the village shop and who had all lost their husbands during the Great War. One of them was the organist, her favourite hymn being 'Rescue the perishing, Care for the dying, Snatch them in Pity from Sin and the grave.' Irene could never understand why she should choose such a hymn for a class of small children, but it obviously made a lasting impression on her, for she remembered it until her dying day.

The Sunday School Anniversary, always the third Sunday in June, was celebrated in two wagons next to the chapel, and they always had the Reepham Band to play. In Irene's memory it was nearly always a fine, sunny day, but there was one exception when a thunderstorm broke out while they were having their tea in the break between afternoon and evening service. Irene was always afraid of thunder, and she couldn't understand the bandsman who

said, "I don't mind the thunder – it's the lightning I don't like."
"What a stupid man," she thought.

They always had a visitor to conduct the Anniversary service, and one year they invited a Salvation Army lady who lived in Norwich. She was not allowed to spend money on public transport on a Sunday, so Father went to Norwich to fetch her. When the collection had been taken she said it was not enough and insisted they take the collecting bags round again. The chapel folk were highly indignant, for they knew the people had given what they could afford in the first place. She was not invited again.

As with so many other things, Royal also held firm opinions on political matters and, when a General Election was in the offing, he took every opportunity to deck his vehicles out in the Liberal Party colours. On one occasion he learned the ghastly news that the son of his solicitor was standing as a Labour candidate. This was too much for Royal to stomach, and he promptly changed his solicitor. Unfortunately, however, he had failed to check the background of his new adviser, a well-known Norwich lawyer with chambers in Queen Street. Nobody had the heart to tell him that his new man was a Tory!

In the last reference to children in his meticulously written memoirs prior to the move to Swannington, Royal defined them as being four in number. Then, after recording the spending of a lot of money on repair work and such things as making up roads and planting trees, he comes up with this priceless gem:

"Nothing outstanding had happened except that our family kept increasing to 10."

Then, within the next couple of pages, we are told that "two more children were born, making a family of 10."

A slight mathematical error at that point, it seems, but there is no disputing the fact that, by the time Royal called a halt to his procreative activities, the grand total stood at 14, and this presented certain problems, especially as regards the matter of transport. A pony and trap would have been of little use to such a large family, but Royal was equal to the occasion. He bought a vehicle which soon became a part of local folklore – a 14-seater charabanc. It was built in the traditional bulbous shape with brass fittings and a canvas hood and sides which were fastened by press studs, and it was painted a rather pleasing shade of green. Then, inscribed on the back in beautiful gold lettering, it bore the name

Woodland Rose, which Royal had given it to denote its stable of origin, and then his name.

The charabanc was purchased from the highly-regarded Holt garage proprietor Alfred Elsden, who delivered it to Swannington. Royal then naturally drove Mr Elsden back to Holt, but first he rounded up his children to get on board for a ride. This was probably a risky decision, for it was the time when vehicles had to be 'run in' at the start of their lives, before being returned to the suppliers after a specified mileage for necessary adjustments to be made. All went well until they reached Edgefield Hill, but then *Woodland Rose* stubbornly refused to go any further, and it was a question of 'all out and push.'

From then on, the vehicle became a familiar sight as it carried out its function throughout the surrounding part of the county – but not always in the same guise.

Royal was nothing if not a canny character and, when he made the purchase, he ensured that *Woodland Rose* could serve as a carrier for stock as well as people. The charabanc body could, with only minimal difficulty, be removed and replaced with what can best be described as the body of a lorry. Thus, it was possible for him to deliver a load of pigs to market in the morning, return home and give it a good scrub out, put on the charabanc part, and it was ready for human passengers. In the guise of a lorry, *Woodland Rose* was a regular part of the Norwich Cattle Market scene on Saturdays whilst, throughout the summer, particularly after harvest, she was out in her full glory running trips around the coast and providing transport for such functions as bowls and darts clubs outings.

For many years she made her stately way around the countryside, but nothing lasts forever, and this was very much the case with *Woodland Rose.* As time went by, she gradually began to show an increasing reluctance to climb hills, and the occasions when it was necessary for passengers to get out and give her a helping hand became steadily more frequent.

I suppose it was one Summer evening, when the family were returning from a visit to their grandparents at Bawdeswell, that the death knell really sounded. All was going well until they started travelling down Lenwade Hill, but then they were horrified to see one of their wheels overtake them and go hurtling down the hill ahead of them.

Even then, however, she was not made redundant – it was rather more of a change of occupation, for she saw out the rest of her years as a shelter for the men as they engaged in such tasks as harvesting swedes or chopping out beet.

III – The Rebel

At this stage in the Royal Cooper story one could be forgiven for thinking that he and his clan were going through life in a state of rural bliss, something resembling a Norfolk version of *The Darling Buds of May*.

This state of affairs, however, was under threat from all directions, steadily driving agriculture into the depressed state which marked the period between the two world wars. Royal felt this as much as anybody, for he had bought more acreage in the form of Folkard's Farm when it had come up for sale as part of the Hackford Hall Estate. The tithe on this land was ten shillings an acre and that on the Swannington farm 7s. 3d.

"Then," he said, "times rapidly got worse and tithes became too heavy a burden for me to bear, so, naturally, when the Norfolk Tithepayers' Association was formed, I was one of the first members on the committee." Hence, it was this tithe business that had first got him into trouble with the authorities.

Originally, when the tithe system was first introduced, it was paid in kind – one tenth of all their produce and stock – every tenth pig, every tenth sheaf of corn. But, farmers being wily characters, they found ways of secreting some of the stuff away so that it wasn't seen. Then, when the tithe had all been settled up, they would repair to the local hostelry and celebrate with their traditional jingle:

We've fooled the parson, we'll fool him again.
Why should the Vicar have one in ten?

Later, however, it was a question of paying in cash terms, and for those who either couldn't or wouldn't pay (and Royal was one who wouldn't) there were compulsory sales of their stock. I have met a number of people who told me they have been to these compulsory sales and seen cattle knocked down for as little as a penny a head, simply because the farmers all got together and agreed not to bid against each other. When the authorities had collected as much money as they could, that was the end of the matter. Eventually, when the heat was off, the farmers would sell the stock back to their troubled colleague for the penny they had paid for it. By that simple ruse, all parties were satisfied.

Many people have told me that Royal Cooper was put into Thorpe Mental Hospital because of his refusal to pay tithes; to make an example of him and to keep him quiet. I found this difficult to accept, but then I recalled that many young girls who brought an illegitimate child into the world had been put into mental asylums, many of them for the rest of their lives.

On the other hand, the authorities had their own ways of dealing with these matters, one of which was to declare the non-payer bankrupt, and this is how they dealt with Royal. In his case it was for what would now be regarded as the paltry sum of £67.12.8d, but it also involved the impounding of furniture and household effects until the money was paid. I cannot think that Royal paid up – I think I detect the hands of his sons in paying it off and getting his bankruptcy lifted.

So his committal to Thorpe Asylum was in no way connected with non-payment of tithes, and the fact that he was shut away for little short of six years indicated a somewhat more serious brush with the authorities. I then recalled Jack's words as he handed over to me the suitcase packed with his father's papers.

"You'll find the answers to all your questions in there," he had said.

I re-opened the case and again started reading its contents, gradually becoming filled with remorse and sadness at what I was reading. Though I had never known the man, I had already developed a great affection for him, in spite of the failings which led him into so much trouble. Firstly, there was his hyperactive brain, which caused him to develop all sorts of controversial religious beliefs contrary to the tenets of the established Church. Allied to this was a broad streak of natural Norfolk cussedness which took over and made his body do things that were completely foreign to his nature. Thus it was that, in the early weeks of 1936, he suffered a severe cerebral attack, during the course of which he became so violent that it took the combined force of three members of the local constabulary to restrain him.

He records the occasion and its consequences in these words:

In the early Spring of 1936 I had what can be regarded as a brainstorm. I was sent to St. Andrew's mental hospital and detained for a few months. I soon recovered and my mind was opened to the heathen doctrine of priestcraft. I was determined to express my views in public and went to Norwich with the object

172

of hiring St. Andrew's Hall for the purpose. I was handed over to the police and sent to the Hellesdon Mental Hospital and, after some months, to St. Andrew's.

I should add that, in between these happenings, he had vented his spleen on the *Eastern Daily Press,* because he wanted them to publish his writings and his interpretation of the Scriptures, but it was very controversial stuff – not exactly *EDP* material – and they refused to print it. He took umbrage over this and, making his way to London Street, made his feelings known by smashing the windows of the Press Office, for which he was hauled up before the magistrates and fined. He refused to pay the fine, and Jack remembers having to go up to the Shirehall to pay it for him.

So Royal found himself "shut away", little knowing at the time that six years were to pass before he would be considered safe enough to regain his place in society. It would be trite to describe it as the saddest period in his life, for that could have been said of almost anybody in such circumstances. But Royal was a man of the open air, farming 500 acres and carrying with him a love for everything around him. He likened it to six years of having been in prison; six years of sadness and utter misery; and he tried all manner of ways of getting back his freedom. On one occasion he drew up a list of 27 people, all well-known to him, with the request that they should be consulted as to their opinion of his mental condition. They were all respected figures in local society – farmers, a solicitor and a police superintendent among them – but it was all to no avail, and it reached the point where he felt completely and utterly deserted, even by those nearest and dearest to him.

It was then, on September 12th 1940, that he wrote one of the saddest letters I have ever read. It was to his youngest child, a little girl named Ann, and, although I am not sure of her age at the time, she was certainly not old enough to read it. It was obviously written for other eyes:

Dear Ann, I'm looking forward to seeing you and the others – how did you like the choc roll? Ma says you don't like nuts – well, that shows you're not such a monkey as your Daddy.

I want you to tell your mother that you want me at home, especially as there is a war on which is likely to get worse as the time goes on. Just fancy, your father has been shut away from home for almost 4 years because some people are afraid of truth and right.

I hardly know how to write to a little girl. Ma told me your doll was in hospital with a broken head – I've been in prison with a broken heart.

Is this a democratic country? I heard Mr Churchill speak last evening, and I wondered what he meant by liberty and justice or if he knew that an Englishman is denied all the things he said we were fighting for.

I know this is all too old for you and Betty but, as you can't read, someone will read it to you, and it will explain itself in the years to come. Tell your Ma to be a wife as well as a mother – then we shall soon meet again this side of the river.

Love to you all,
Micky
xxxxx

A sad letter, indeed, with a degree of unhappiness matched only by the strangeness of the manner in which the grieving father signed it. Why Micky? For reasons now unknown, it seems that, though the children were brought up to show unfailing respect to their elders, it was the accustomed practice for them to address Royal and Olive as Micky and Daisy respectively. The Cooper family are full of surprises!

Meanwhile, in spite of Royal's rebellious activity, he was never at any time regarded as being insane, with the result that he was given a reasonable amount of freedom. Jack used to go to Thorpe and collect him for the occasional weekend and take him back on Monday, and Royal was allowed to go out for country walks around Thorpe, as were many of the other patients.

Furthermore, there was some kind of agreement between the Medical Superintendent and the patients that, if they could get away from the hospital and support themselves entirely unaided for a certain length of time – about a fortnight, I believe – they would not be brought back. Not surprisingly, Royal had several attempts at this, but without success, although there was one occasion when he did almost succeed. He got away and went back to Woodlands, his own farm, but obviously he avoided going into the buildings or the house. The family never even knew he was there. When he had first taken over Woodlands Farm there had been a little beck that used to wind through the far end of the farm, and there he had planted a lot of trees, which had become, if not exactly a wood, at least a little copse, and that is where he took refuge. He had little difficulty in supporting himself without going in any of the buildings, for he knew where the vegetables grew, and he knew where the hens laid their eggs. Then, unknown to his family, it was his custom every morning to go to the edge of his copse and peer through and watch his young children going off to school and then coming back in the afternoons. The feeling of anguish in his troubled mind at those times can only be imagined.

One big trouble about his being incarcerated in such a place as a mental asylum was that he had too much time on his hands, and this did him no good at all, for his brain was ever-active, ever-enquiring. He wrote:

"I've always taken a great interest in theology, politics and such things, and it was while in Thorpe Mental Hospital that I learned more about these subjects than I could ever have hoped to. I have studied the Science of Life and come to conclusions contrary to tradition and I am convinced I have got the key to the Scriptures."

He did a tremendous amount of work, and he wrote a thesis, running to around 200 closely-typed pages, which was his interpretation of the Scriptures. He called it "The Science of Life or The Second Coming of Christ." I have not read it all, but he did a slightly abridged version which I have studied, and I have to say that I am inclined to agree with a certain amount of what he says. However, he took things very much to extremes. He had no time for organised religion – he referred to his dislike of the Bishops and their "black puttees" and, as he put it, "parsons perpetually dressed in black as though they live in a world of darkness and superstition." Then there was the dog collar – "a collar worn the wrong way round," he said, which suggested, to him at least, that they didn't know which way they were going.

A calmer state of mind would surely have told him that making such remarks about the Church of England could hardly endear him to its adherents or make them very keen on what he was writing.

He sent a copy of his manuscript to the Archbishop of Canterbury. I doubt whether the Archbishop ever read it. I doubt whether he even read the covering letter. I certainly hope not, for I have read it and can think of only one word to describe it, and that is "scurrilous."

Later on, he went even further and sent a copy to the Prime Minister who, at that time, was Harold Wilson. He waited a month and got no reply, so he wrote again, in the following terms:

"To the Prime Minister. I am an Englishman and, as such, claim the right to have my book 'The Science of Life or The Second Coming of Christ' printed and published in this country, my country. You have a copy – what have you done with it? Put it on the fire?" He went on and on in similar vein and ended with the question, "How much longer are we to be made fools of by a British government?" Then he signed it "Royal W.J. Cooper" and added a delightful little postscript: "Best Wishes to Mrs Wilson."

He also sent a copy of the manuscript to Ted Heath, who was Leader of the Opposition at the time, and received a very polite reply, although it was readily apparent that Mr Heath had never even read it.

IV – The Poet

One part of Royal Cooper's life which, unlike his religious investigations, did derive benefit from his long stay in Thorpe Hospital was his poetry. Even from the days of his youth he had derived great pleasure from versifying, and he had gained a reputation for being able to run off a poem in a matter of minutes. All of them still exist, in manuscript form, in that Aladdin's Cave of a suitcase with all his other documents, and it is interesting to contrast the almost child-like simplicity of his early efforts with the more meticulous style of his maturity. During his six years of detention he had time to work on the form and structure of his poems and the sentiments he was expressing, and some of them were remarkably good.

Bearing in mind the nature of the man, it is probably not surprising that much of his output was religious in content, and those of his readers who shared that interest could certainly never complain of being given short shrift. At least 20 or 30 verses would flow from his pen as he put his message across.

At the other end of the spectrum, Royal revelled in the occasional burst of humorous verse, as in the tribute to Bob Dyball on a previous page. Then there was the meeting of the Reepham Branch of the National Farmers' Union, at a time when the agricultural industry was in a parlous state. It was, of course, purely coincidental that an Election was in the offing, but the

Chairman stressed the great honour being afforded to members by
the two Members of Parliament who were coming from
Westminster to address them. This was how Royal recorded the
event:

> "Yes, Reepham has been honoured,"
> That's what the Chairman said!
> By two M.P.s who came to please
> An industry near dead.
>
> This industry, as all well know,
> Is in a sorry plight;
> So Mr X and Mr Y
> Came down to put it right.
>
> They talked as all the M.P.s can
> Of barley, beer and beet,
> And said that they the rot would stay
> And put them on their feet.
>
> The farmers cheered and said Hear! Hear!
> These chaps the tale can tell,
> And, though their heads were in the air,
> Their feet were still in Hell.
>
> They promise this, they promise that,
> Like clouds without the rain.
> They promise you great things to do
> If you send them back again.
>
> This job is just another stunt
> Before the next Election.
> They come to Town your thoughts to drown
> And save you from dejection.
>
> Yes, Reepham has been honoured,
> Just as the Chairman said,
> By two M.P.s who came to tease
> An Industry now dead.

The poems of Royal Cooper which gave me the greatest
personal pleasure, however, were the descriptive pieces, and there

was one amongst that group which, apart from the beauty of its words, drew my attention for a very special reason.

During the latter years of the 1930s, as I stumbled along from youth to manhood, we lived in Thorpe St Andrew, that sedate village much coveted by Norwich yet steadfastly resisting the city's blandishments and maintaining its rural charm. Thorpe included a collection of beauty spots, one of our favourites for Sunday afternoon and Summer evening strolls being Postwick Grove. There, the rabbits would scuttle from human approach across the marshy meadows while cattle drank their fill from the brink of the nearby river.

Yes, we were fond of Postwick Grove, as also were the hospital patients who could usually be seen passing that way on their daily constitutionals. Firstly, there were the 'loners', moving with measured tread at pre-determined and never-varying speed, each one alone in his own private world. Then there were those who, though similarly unbending, would allow themselves the occasional luxury of "Morning, Master" as they passed another walker. Finally, there were the more outgoing patients, the ones who were not walking merely for exercise but who were ever ready to stop and 'spend the time of day' with the villagers. We always talked to the patients, for we had been told that it was 'good for them.'

One man who came into that category was Royal Cooper himself, for he was a great lover of that particular beauty spot. It was when I was sorting out the poetical manuscripts from his suitcase that I became aware of the fact. One by one I looked at the titles of the various pieces, deciding which to read forthwith and which to put on one side for later perusal. Then it happened. I picked up a rough sheet of paper, adorned like all the others with that splendid copper plate writing of his, and glanced at the title. What I saw sent a kind of shockwave throughout my system, for the two words were "Postwick Grove."

I avidly read through the verses, and my mind was immediately carried back to those heady days of youth. I have no idea what fate may have befallen that favourite beauty spot in the intervening years, but I am firmly of the belief that anybody who had known Postwick Grove in the thirties would have seen the place again through the evocative lines that Royal had so meticulously conjured up.

Postwick Grove

O'er hills and vales where e'er we rove,
On marshy plain or river's brink,
Beneath the shades of Postwick Grove
We'll rest awhile to gaze and think.

Familiar objects meet our view,
A church's spire, a chimney tall,
The stately old mixed in the new
Past generations to recall.

The river in the valley flows
With placid calm and noiseless trills.
A giant oak beside it grows
With arms outstretched towards the hills.

The cattle graze on marshy plain;
At river's brink they drink their fill,
And by their lives man's life sustain
With flowing milk, and hide and grill.

O'er hills and vales where e'er we rove,
On marshy plain or river's brink,
Beneath the shades of Postwick Grove
We'll rest awhile to view and think.

And though man violates the scene
With iron rails and pylons tall,
And warplanes break the calm serene,
Yet Nature's voice to Nature call.

Man is of Nature but a part,
Yet from that part he strays to fall.
At Postwick Grove again take heart,
Nature is God and Lord of All.

But then my mind jumped ahead of me. I have always regretted
the fact that I never knew Royal Cooper in his lifetime, but was
that really so? Could he possibly have been one of the patients I
had seen taking his constitutional? Could he, indeed, have been

one of those with whom we would 'spend the time of day' as our paths crossed? Whatever the truth of the matter, it's a pleasing thought.

V – The Happy ending

It was in the latter part of 1941, just as Royal was coming to the end of his sixth year of incarceration, that the decision was made to give him back his freedom. I know not why the decision was made at that time, for he certainly had no intention of giving up his contentious beliefs, but perhaps the fact that he had by then reached his sixties led them to hope that he would henceforth decide to keep them more to himself.

Be that as it may, one can only imagine the emotions he must have felt at the thought of resuming his old life amidst the people who had been such a big part of his earlier years. At last he would be free of the restrictions of hospital routine – free to go back to his extensive family and friends at the Home Farm at Woodlands. What a celebration they would have!

But it was not to be. Unpredictable as ever, Royal declined to go home. Well aware, as he was, of the trouble and torment that he had brought upon his family, he was unable to bring himself to face them. But, at the same time, independent as always, there was the need to support himself. Hence, though no longer a young man, he found employment as a labourer, helping to lay out Foulsham airfield. Even there, it seems, he was unable to avoid controversy, for he soon found himself at odds with his workmates, who actually accused him of working too hard!

Whilst working at Foulsham he 'lived' in a barn at Whitwell. I use the word 'lived' somewhat loosely for, although the owners made great efforts to entice him indoors for a hot meal, he preferred to remain outside, even to the extent of sleeping in the barn.

All the while, he was unable to bring himself to face the family, but eventually he managed to brace himself and he went home to Woodlands Farm, the place which, in his estimation, was second only to Heaven itself. There he set about resuming what, for him at least, was a normal life. On a personal note, I recall the great surge of pleasure that I experienced when, rummaging through Royal's old suitcase, I came across a posed photograph of sixteen people. In front were an elderly lady and gentleman – Royal and

The Cooper Family Reunion

Olive Cooper – and behind them were 7 men and 7 women – the family, reunited – and all with smiling faces.

The very sight of that photograph meant that the sad story I had to tell would, at least, lead me to a happy ending.

For Royal himself, the days of extensive farming were now over, and eventually Jack and Etta moved into Woodlands. Folkard's Farm (known by then as Jordan's Farm) was sold, and it was then that Royal bought Church Farm at Felthorpe. Then, in 1960, he published the little book which, many years later, was to capture my imagination on the shelf of Allan Thompson's bookshop in Wymondham.

Royal did his own publishing and engaged in such advertising matters as he could, though these were mainly restricted to erecting a notice by his gate and engaging in sales to callers at his door. As luck would have it, however, the folk at the *Eastern Daily Press* seem to have forgotten his earlier misdemeanour when he smashed their office windows. They sent a reporter and photographer to Felthorpe and, in due course, they published a photograph of him and a little story, which ran:

'We have become accustomed to farmers selling their produce at the farm gates, but here is a farmer selling a different kind of produce.'

And there was the picture of Royal outside his gate at Church Farm and a sign erected by the side of the gate saying " 'Poems and Proverbs' by Royal W.J. Cooper, available here, price nine shillings and sixpence (By post 10s. 3d.)"

A few years later he sold Church Farm and bought Hill House at Horsford, where he was destined to live for the rest of his life. All the while, to the extreme discomfort of his family, he maintained his absolute obsession with his religious beliefs. However, time and his earlier experiences had mellowed him, and he had learned the lesson that gentle persuasion was likely to be more productive than scurrilous verbal abuse. For the final twelve years he contented himself with proclamations of his beliefs by means of hoardings erected outside his house. There was always the chance that a passer-by might read and share his thoughts.

He had further mellowed to the extent of enjoying an occasional game of cards – though only on a strictly non-gambling basis with Felthorpe Whist Drive Club.

It was in 1975, having reached the highly respectable age of 95, that Royal Cooper departed this life.

Royal selling his books 'at the farm gate.'

Felthorpe Whist Drive Club Outing

Family Group at Royal and Olive's Golden Wedding.

The coming of the third generation.

Royal Cooper at 90.

I rather wish I had known him in life, but I am grateful to the many people, particularly his family, who at least enabled me to get to know him in death. And they were all so effusive in their praise of the man – never have I heard a single word spoken against him.

There was the lady who described him as "a real country gent, and his wife was a lady," and another who recalled him, more simply, as "a damn nice chap." Then there was my late friend Jack Pull, a male nurse who tended him during his years in Thorpe Hospital, and who treasured the copy of the book which Royal had given him in 1960. "Royal Cooper," he said, "was one of nature's gentlemen."

What better epitaph could any man ask than to go to his grave to the accompaniment of such loving praise from his peers? For my part, however, I prefer to end my story of his life with a few lines of his own writing:

An Evening Prayer

The evening shadows round us fall
As Earth the Sun doth hide,
And we, Thy children, to Thee call
And ask Thee to abide.

Abide with us that we may feel
Thy power to guide and keep;
Protect us through the coming night
And guard us while we sleep.

Our Life as day ebbs to its close,
Our sun at evening sets;
Grant us this night a sweet repose
Without a day's regrets,

That we may greet the coming morn,
If morn we live to see,
With minds and bodies all reborn
To live and work for Thee.

Acknowledgements

This book owes much to the many old friends who have so willingly shared both memories and photographs with me. Those in the first group are too numerous to mention, but for assistance with illustrations I am particularly indebted to Rhoda Bunn, Joan Darby, Ted Fowler, David Little, Philip Standley and Philip Yaxley.

A special word of appreciation goes to the family of Royal Cooper for their whole-hearted support and encouragement which enabled me to record the chequered life and times of that troubled man – a story I have long wanted to write.

Bob Bagshaw,
Wymondham,
May 2002.

The wild flower illustrations are reproduced from 'Familiar Wild Flowers' by F. Edward Hulme, F.L.S., F.S.A., published in sixpenny weekly parts in 1877.